PLAY OR DEFEND?

68 Hands to Test Your Bridge Skill

Julian Pottage

Master Point Press

Master Point Press
331 Douglas Ave.
Toronto, Ontario Canada
M5M 1H2
(416) 781-0351 Fax (416) 781-1831
Internet www.masterpointpress.com

Canadian Cataloguing in Publication Data
Pottage Julian
Play or defend?/ Julian Pottage.

ISBN 1-894154-55-X

1. Contract bridge — Dummy play. 2. Contract bridge — Defensive play. I. Title.

GV1282.3.P673 2003 2002   795.41'53   C2003-9000087-7

Editor	Ray Lee
Cover and interior design	Olena S. Sullivan
Interior format and copyediting	Deanna Bourassa

Printed and bound in Canada by Webcom Canada Ltd.

1 2 3 4 5 6 7   06 05 04 03

CONTENTS

BONUS QUESTIONS

INTRODUCTION

Some seven or eight years ago, Andrew Diosy and the Lees came up with a novel and effective way to present interesting bridge problems. This was to display the four players' hands at the outset and to break the answer into halves. This not only means that more people can enjoy the problems, because exposing all four hands makes both declaring and defending easier, but it also gives readers a second chance to find the solution. Having observed that this format would suit many of my best deals, Ray and I discussed the possibility of a new book – and here you can see the result: 'Play or Defend?'.

The book comes in three sections, arranged in increasing level of difficulty. Within each section, I have broadly followed the same principle, although with minor variations to avoid similar themes appearing in clusters. In the 'Fairly Easy' batch, you need not spend overly long searching for pretty squeeze endings. Similarly, with the 'Tougher Still' group, if you think that a simple hold-up at Trick 1 solves the problem, you have almost certainly overlooked something.

On more or less every hand, I have included a Standard American bidding sequence, with conventional bids explained. This provides the option, should you wish to challenge yourself, of initially studying only two players' hands. For someone with the right combination of technical and analytical skills, every hand is soluble with the sight of only two hands (plus, in some cases, knowing what happens on the first few tricks). As the declarer can succeed in over 70% of the contracts, I suggest that you start looking at the North-South cards. If you quickly decide that you would rather defend, I recommend taking the West seat on any odd-numbered deal and the East seat on the even numbers. Whilst defeating a contract tends to involve partnership cooperation, normally one of the defenders has a greater role than the other. I have arranged for the defeatable contracts to match this order. I have not stated the vulnerability on any deal. If you think that the bidding is only reasonable under the right conditions, assume they exist. The scoring is always teams or rubber, so forget about overtricks.

Several people have commented on how original they find my material. Without giving away too many trade secrets, I am happy to give a brief insight into how it is done. You will find that I have based roughly half the deals in this book on ideas that have come to me or on hands that I have played. Of the remainder, a third derive from themes that I have bumped into by accident, often by checking other ideas using Bill Bailey's *Deep Finesse* program. I make a point of only using subject matter from an external source if I believe that I can genuinely improve the original setting. Typically, I may adjust a few of the cards to make the bidding, contract, lead or early play more reasonable. I might also edit out an alternative solution or make the winning one both more logical and less dependent on an apparently contrived lie of the cards.

Although I prepared all the hands and text myself, others have contributed along the way. As well as those mentioned above, I would like to thank Graham Allan, Hugh Darwen and Maureen Dennison, who helped greatly in checking the proofs. If I may, perhaps I can finish with a word of advice. Try not to read too many hands at a time. After all, you would hardly down a whole bottle of vintage bourbon in one sitting. Besides, it may take me a while to collect enough material for a sequel!

Julian Pottage
September 2002

SECTION 1

Fairly
Easy

HAND 1 DIRECT ACTION

♠ A 5
♡ A K 8 5
◇ J 10 8 5 4
♣ J 8

♠ K J 8 7 4
♡ 10 6
◇ A Q 6
♣ Q 10 3

♠ 10 6
♡ J 9 4 2
◇ 3 2
♣ 9 7 6 5 4

♠ Q 9 3 2
♡ Q 7 3
◇ K 9 7
♣ A K 2

W	N	E	S
			1♣
1♠	dbl[1]	pass	1NT
pass	3NT	all pass	

1. Negative.

Contract: 3NT
Opening Lead: ♠7

HAND 2 ACHILLES' HEEL

♠ A 9 8 5
♡ Q J 5 3
◇ Q J 10
♣ K 4

♠ K 10 7 2
♡ 8 7 2
◇ A 8
♣ 9 6 5 2

♠ Q 3
♡ K 10 6 4
◇ K 6 5 2
♣ 10 7 3

♠ J 6 4
♡ A 9
◇ 9 7 4 3
♣ A Q J 8

W	N	E	S
			1♣
pass	1♡	pass	1NT
pass	2◇[1]	pass	2NT
pass	3NT	all pass	

1. Checkback asking for 3♡/4♠.

Contract: 3NT
Opening Lead: ♠2

HAND 1 DIRECT ACTION

Suppose you win the ten of spades with the queen, go across to dummy with a heart, and run the ◇ J. West wins with the queen and plays a spade to dummy's bare ace. You will then go down, losing three spades and two diamonds.

Ducking the first trick works no better. East returns a spade and West, with both diamond entries, can still get the suit going.

Since the defensive strength lies mainly in one hand, perhaps you might think of an endplay or squeeze. The problem is this: with the hearts not breaking kindly, you have only seven top tricks. Therefore, a single extra winner generated using one of these methods will scarcely help.

Can you find a way to make the contract? See page 86 for the second part of the solution.

HAND 2 ACHILLES' HEEL

Going up with dummy's ace of spades will not work because the resulting blockage will be merely temporary. East can win the first diamond and cash the spade queen. The defenders will score three spades and two diamonds.

Playing low at Trick 1 seems more obvious and the queen wins. If East returns a spade, the contract makes. North's nine will take care of the fourth round of spades and declarer can take the winning heart finesse after setting up the diamonds.

Is the contract always cold, or can the right switch at Trick 2 kill it? See page 86 for the second part of the solution.

HAND 3 TENS AND NINES

```
            ♠ A 10 2
            ♡ J 9 5
            ◇ 10 9 6 4
            ♣ A 10 9
♠ Q J 9 7              ♠ 8 4
♡ K 8 3        N       ♡ Q 10 7 2
◇ K J 8 7   W     E    ◇ Q 3
♣ 6 5          S       ♣ 8 7 4 3 2
            ♠ K 6 5 3
            ♡ A 6 4
            ◇ A 5 2
            ♣ K Q J
```

W	N	E	S
			1NT
pass	3NT	all pass	

Contract: 3NT
Opening Lead: ♠Q

HAND 4 ENTRY EFFICIENCY

```
            ♠ 10 6
            ♡ 9 8 4
            ◇ J 8 6 5 2
            ♣ 10 9 3
♠ 8 3                 ♠ 5 2
♡ Q J 6 2      N      ♡ A 10 7 5 3
◇ 10 9 7 3  W     E   ◇ A Q
♣ 8 5 2        S      ♣ K Q 7 4
            ♠ A K Q J 9 7 4
            ♡ K
            ◇ K 4
            ♣ A J 6
```

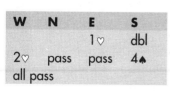

W	N	E	S
		1♡	dbl
2♡	pass	pass	4♠
all pass			

Contract: 4♠
Opening Lead: ♡Q

HAND 3 TENS AND NINES

It looks right to win the opening lead with the king, saving the ace-ten as a tenace over the jack. Unless spades break 3-3, you will need two diamond tricks, so perhaps you duck a diamond at Trick 2. If you do that, East wins with the queen and switches to a low heart. West's king wins this and, when the ten covers the nine on the next round, you hold up the ace of hearts once more. East now abandons hearts and sends back a diamond. This destroys any chance of a squeeze and, when neither pointed suit divides evenly, you go one down.

You might think of finessing the ten of spades at Trick 2 to start diamonds from dummy. Unfortunately that does not work either. This time the defenders have a choice of winning actions. The most obvious one is probably for West to win the diamond, switch to a heart now and then revert to spades after the second round of hearts. You lose two hearts, two diamonds and a spade.

Can you see a better way to play the hand? See page 87 for the second part of the solution.

HAND 4 ENTRY EFFICIENCY

East goes up with the ace of hearts and returns the suit, South ruffing. Success here depends on making a diamond trick as well as two clubs. The opening bid and West's weak raise mark East with most of the missing strength, which means that the cards should lie well for declarer. Even so, entries present a problem. There is no way to lead clubs twice and diamonds once from dummy when it contains only one obvious entry, the ♠10. Nor can you arrange for the defenders to make helpful leads. They possess an ample supply of exit cards in hearts.

Maybe you could create one extra entry by ruffing the heart return high and finessing the ♠6. When you do get to dummy, which finesse should you take? See page 87 for the second part of the solution.

HAND 5 BATH TIME BLUES

```
                        ♠ 6 4
                        ♡ J 9
                        ◊ K Q 10 9 7 2
                        ♣ A K 6
     ♠ K Q 10 8 2              ♠ 9 7 3
     ♡ Q 10 7 4          N     ♡ K 5 3
     ◊ J 4           W       E ◊ A 6 5
     ♣ J 4               S     ♣ 7 5 3 2
                        ♠ A J 5
                        ♡ A 8 6 2
                        ◊ 8 3
                        ♣ Q 10 9 8
```

W	N	E	S
	1◊	pass	1♡
pass	2◊	pass	2NT
pass	3NT	all pass	

Contract   3NT
Opening Lead: ♠K

HAND 6 PASS THE PARCEL

```
                        ♠ K 6 4 3
                        ♡ Q 8 2
                        ◊ 10 9
                        ♣ A J 10 3
     ♠ Q 8 7 5                ♠ J 2
     ♡ 10 6 4 3         N     ♡ 9 7 5
     ◊ K 6 5        W       E ◊ A 7 3
     ♣ 9 2               S     ♣ K Q 8 7 5
                        ♠ A 10 9
                        ♡ A K J
                        ◊ Q J 8 4 2
                        ♣ 6 4
```

W	N	E	S
		pass	1NT
pass	2♣	dbl	2◊
pass	3NT	all pass	

Contract: 3NT
Opening Lead: ♣9

HAND 5 BATH TIME BLUES

Clearly, declarer ducks the opening lead since a spade through the jack later will mean losing four spades and the ◇A. West should read the spade position from East's signal and needs to switch. With the ace-king of clubs on view in dummy, the ♡4 looks the natural choice. If the ♡K wins, a heart continuation is no good: declarer ducks and loses merely two hearts, a spade and a diamond. However, East can revert to spades. South can ill afford to go up with the ace, so West scores the ♠Q and then goes back to hearts, leading the queen to squash dummy's jack. In this case the defenders score the five tricks they require: two in each major plus the ◇A.

To succeed declarer must capture the king of hearts with the ace at Trick 2. Yes, East will get in with the ◇A and can play back a heart, but the eight stops the fourth round of the suit and the contract makes. Does the story end here or can the defenders do better? See page 88 for the second part of the solution.

HAND 6 PASS THE PARCEL

In kitchen-bridge style, Trick 1 would go nine, ten, queen, small. Seeing no immediate future in clubs (indeed leading up to the ace-jack would concede an overtrick), East shifts to a heart. West can do no better than to take the first diamond and lead another club. In this case, playing either the ace or low from dummy leaves East with no way to get the clubs going and leaves declarer plenty of time to set up the diamonds and make the contract.

Foreseeing the above, perhaps East allows the ♣10 to hold. Now if declarer goes after diamonds, West wins the first round with the king and continues clubs, this time with dummy's A-J-x totally exposed. Nothing can prevent East from clearing the clubs and, upon getting in with the ◇A, running the suit. Does this mean 3NT should fail or can declarer produce an effective counter? See page 88 for the second part of the solution.

HAND 7 TEN-TON TRUCK

```
                              ♠ 10 2
                              ♡ Q J
                              ◇ A K J 10 9 3
                              ♣ 10 8 2
        ♠ 9 6 5 3                              ♠ J 4
        ♡ A 6              ┌─────────┐          ♡ K 10 8 7 5 2
        ◇ 6 4             │    N    │          ◇ 8 5 2
        ♣ Q 9 7 5 3      │ W     E │          ♣ J 6
                          │    S    │
                          └─────────┘
                              ♠ A K Q 8 7
                              ♡ 9 4 3
                              ◇ Q 7
                              ♣ A K 4
```

W	N	E	S
			1♠
pass	2◇	pass	3♣
pass	3◇	pass	4◇
pass	4♠	all pass	

Contract: 4♠
Opening Lead: ♣5

HAND 8 ACHIEVING ACCESS

```
                              ♠ Q 8 6
                              ♡ J 8 7
                              ◇ 7 5 4 3
                              ♣ K Q 10
        ♠ 10 7 4 2                           ♠ K 9 3
        ♡ 5 3              ┌─────────┐         ♡ A Q 4
        ◇ Q J 10          │    N    │         ◇ K 8
        ♣ 9 7 3 2        │ W     E │         ♣ J 8 6 5 4
                          │    S    │
                          └─────────┘
                              ♠ A J 5
                              ♡ K 10 9 6 2
                              ◇ A 9 6 2
                              ♣ A
```

W	N	E	S
		1♣	1♡
pass	2♡	pass	4♡
all pass			

Contract: 4♡
Opening Lead: ◇Q

HAND 7 TEN‑TON TRUCK

East covers dummy's ♣8 with the jack and you surely want to win the first trick. Having done so, you could cash three rounds of trumps and then turn to diamonds. This would work either if trumps break 3-3 or if the defender with four trumps holds three diamonds. Neither wish comes true and West ruffs the third round of diamonds, leaving you with three further losers in hand.

Since dummy contains a doubleton heart, perhaps you think about a heart ruff. The defenders may choose how to counter heart plays. East can win and return a club (leaving you with three top losers and a slow trump loser), or West can shift to a diamond, threatening to cut you off from the table.

Your options seem to be running out. Is there something else you can do? See page 89 for the second part of the solution.

HAND 8 ACHIEVING ACCESS

If East fails to overtake with the king, life becomes simple. For example, you win with the ◊A, cash the ♣A and exit with a diamond. Probably you will get a club return and then you could discard two diamonds and play on trumps. East can hop up with the ace but cannot exit safely.

Suppose now that the ◊K appears. If you win this, cash the ♣A and exit with a diamond, West scores two tricks and gets off play with a spade. Unless East does something daft, you are bound to lose another trick as well as the ♡A. Therefore again you hope that East has a doubleton diamond, and duck.

You win the second diamond and it seems natural to unblock the ♣A straight away. If you concede a diamond, that would transpose to the losing line in the previous paragraph. You will have to broach one of the majors and neither looks appealing. Can you make the contract from here? See page 89 for the second part of the solution.

HAND 9 DELICATE DIAMONDS

```
                              ♠ A 10 9 6
                              ♡ K J 10 8
                              ◇ J 7 6
                              ♣ 9 7
           ♠ J 3                              ♠ K Q 5 2
           ♡ 9 7 6 4 2        ┌─────────┐    ♡ 3
           ◇ Q 10 2           │    N    │    ◇ A 9 5 4 3
           ♣ 8 6 3        W   │ W     E │ E  ♣ A 5 2
                              │    S    │
                              └─────────┘
                              ♠ 8 7 4
                              ♡ A Q 5
                              ◇ K 8
                              ♣ K Q J 10 4
```

W	N	E	S
		1◇	1NT
pass	2♣[1]	pass	2◇
pass	3NT	all pass	

1. Stayman.

Contract: 3NT
Opening Lead: ◇2

HAND 10 NULLIFYING NORTH

```
                              ♠ 10 2
                              ♡ A K J 9 5 4 3
                              ◇ K
                              ♣ Q 8 6
           ♠ 7                                ♠ K 5
           ♡ 8 2             ┌─────────┐      ♡ Q 10 7 6
           ◇ 8 7 6 5 2       │    N    │      ◇ A Q 9 3
           ♣ K 10 7 5 4   W  │ W     E │ E    ♣ A J 3
                              │    S    │
                              └─────────┘
                              ♠ A Q J 9 8 6 4 3
                              ♡ —
                              ◇ J 10 4
                              ♣ 9 2
```

W	N	E	S
	1♡	1NT	4♠
all pass			

Contract: 4♠
Opening Lead: ♣5

HAND 9 DELICATE DIAMONDS

Suppose that East, who appears to possess several possible entries, puts up the ace of diamonds and returns the suit. The king takes the second round and declarer knocks out the ♣A. West scores the ◊Q but there the matter rests: 3NT makes with an overtrick. East could switch to a low spade at Trick 2, but that hardly helps. The ace captures West's jack and again declarer sets up the clubs. At least this way the defenders collect four tricks: two spades, a diamond and a club.

East could duck the initial diamond, in which case the eight wins. Again, a blockage results. The ace wins the second round of diamonds and the queen the third.

Can either side do any better? See page 90 for the second part of the solution.

HAND 10 NULLIFYING NORTH

Knowing that West would lead the ten from a suit with 10-9-7-5 at the top, East confidently plays the jack when dummy plays low. It looks normal to continue by laying down the ♣A. The ♣5 could be from a four-card suit, in which case three quick club tricks and the ◊A would save any defensive headaches. In practice, West drops the dreaded ♣4 for under the ace. This not only signifies a five-card suit, but it surely denies a heart void, the ♣10 being the card to signal such a holding.

East could still cash the ◊A and play a spade, hoping that West has something useful in trumps. A bare queen will do, as would J-x-x (impossible on the bidding, of course). J-x combined with a singleton heart would also suffice. Declarer would be unable to cash two hearts to get rid of diamonds and would run into a trump promotion. However, a jump to 4♠ on ace-queen to seven and little else sounds rather frisky.

Can you defeat the contract as the cards lie? See page 90 for the second part of the solution.

HAND 11 USEFUL CONCESSION

```
                          ♠ A K 8 6 5
                          ♡ J 8 5 4
                          ◇ J
                          ♣ A 6 2
         ♠ J 9 7 2                        ♠ 10 4 3
         ♡ A Q 7          ┌──────────┐    ♡ K 9 2
         ◇ 10 8 6 5 4     │    N     │    ◇ Q 9 2
         ♣ 8              │ W      E │    ♣ Q 10 9 3
                          │    S     │
                          └──────────┘
```

W	N	E	S
			1♣
pass	1♠	pass	1NT
pass	2◇¹	pass	2NT
pass	3NT	all pass	

1. Checkback asking for 3♠/4♡.

```
                          ♠ Q
                          ♡ 10 6 3
                          ◇ A K 7 3
                          ♣ K J 7 5 4
```

Contract: 3NT
Opening Lead: ◇5

HAND 12 ANGLE OF ATTACK

```
                          ♠ K 6 5
                          ♡ Q 8 6 4
                          ◇ J
                          ♣ A J 9 6 4
         ♠ 3                              ♠ A Q 7 4
         ♡ J 9 7 5 3      ┌──────────┐    ♡ A 10 2
         ◇ 6 4 2          │    N     │    ◇ 8 7 5
         ♣ K 8 7 5        │ W      E │    ♣ Q 10 2
                          │    S     │
                          └──────────┘
```

W	N	E	S
		1♣	1◇
pass	1NT	pass	2♠
pass	2NT	pass	3♠
pass	4♠	all pass	

```
                          ♠ J 10 9 8 2
                          ♡ K
                          ◇ A K Q 10 9 3
                          ♣ 3
```

Contract: 4♠
Opening Lead: ♡5

HAND 11 USEFUL CONCESSION

You should start by winning the first trick. If you need to lose a trick in one of the black suits and the defenders can cash three hearts, you can ill afford to give up a diamond. To unblock the spades it looks right to cash the ♠Q and suppose you then cross to the ♣A to take two round spades. The miracle layout of J-10-9 tripleton fails to occur and you must try your luck in clubs. The finesse works, but the suit splits 4-1. You now concede a club and, if a diamond comes back, you make the contract. Alas, by this stage, West has had several chances to signal for hearts and in practice East should find the heart switch to put you down one.

Clearing the spades before playing a second round of clubs serves little purpose since dummy contains no further entry once the ♣A has gone. For the same reason, neither would it help to keep one or both of the top spades in dummy. Can you find a way to nine tricks? See page 91 for the second part of the solution.

HAND 12 ANGLE OF ATTACK

East naturally puts up the ♡A, which fells the king. The ♡10 seems a normal return and the queen wins. Declarer might now come to hand with a diamond in order to run the jack of spades. East can counter this by winning with the queen and persisting with the heart attack. It is now a simple matter to wait until the third round of trumps before taking the ace and returning a club. This leaves the lead stranded in dummy.

The bidding and early play makes it almost certain East holds the ♠A to justify an opening bid. Therefore, after winning the heart return at Trick 2, declarer should play a trump from dummy — probably low to cater for a bare ace. East can go in with the queen, continue hearts and hold up the ♠A. However, this time South has a diamond entry and the contract rolls home. Does the story end here or can you find an effective way to play a forcing game? See page 91 for the second part of the solution.

HAND 13 SAFE FINESSING

```
              ♠ A 8
              ♡ A K 9 8 2
              ◇ 10 9 4
              ♣ A K J
♠ K 9 6                      ♠ J 10 7 4 3
♡ 10 7 4        N            ♡ Q J 6 3
◇ K J 7      W     E         ◇ 5
♣ 8 5 4 2       S            ♣ Q 10 6
              ♠ Q 5 2
              ♡ 5
              ◇ A Q 8 6 3 2
              ♣ 9 7 3
```

W	N	E	S
	1♡	pass	1NT
pass	3NT	all pass	

Contract: 3NT
Opening Lead: ♠6

HAND 14 CONQUERING QUEENS

```
              ♠ 5
              ♡ 10 6 5 4 2
              ◇ J 8 7 4
              ♣ Q 4 2
♠ K 10 8 4 2                 ♠ Q 7 6
♡ 8 3           N            ♡ A K J 9 7
◇ Q 3        W     E         ◇ 2
♣ J 8 6 3       S            ♣ K 10 7 5
              ♠ A J 9 3
              ♡ Q
              ◇ A K 10 9 6 5
              ♣ A 9
```

W	N	E	S
		1♡	dbl
1♠	pass	2♠	3◇
pass	4◇	pass	5◇
all pass			

Contract: 5◇
Opening Lead: ♡8

HAND 13 SAFE FINESSING

The obvious play to Trick 1 goes six, eight, ten, queen. Then cross to the
♣A to take a diamond finesse. If West wins and plays a small spade
(allowing for the ♠Q to be a falsecard from Q-J-x), the contract makes
with an overtrick. With the spades blocked, the defenders collect just two
diamonds and a spade. Leading the ♠K to the bare ace works much better. Now the suit will run once West regains the lead in diamonds.

Suppose South ducks the opening lead in both hands. East can return
a spade and West must decide whether to sacrifice the king. It matters
little as dummy's pair of ace-kings stop the rounded suits and East can
never win the third round of spades.

Perhaps East works out that the ♠6 cannot be fourth best and, placing South with ♠K-x-x, switches to the ♡Q at Trick 2. No, that fails as
well. The king wins and, when West continues with a low heart after winning the first diamond, declarer can afford to put up dummy's ♡A to
block the suit. Does this mean the contract should make? See page 92 for
the second part of the solution.

HAND 14 CONQUERING QUEENS

Having won the first heart with the king, East can read the ♡Q as a singleton. South's advance to 5◇ (and takeout double) would seem dubious
actions with two losing hearts. Since the weak dummy and its singleton
spade telegraphs the threat of spade ruffs, East may switch to the ◇2,
South's ace winning.

Declarer may go on to take the ♠A, ruff a spade, return to the ♣A, ruff
a spade, ruff a heart and ruff another spade. Nobody overruffs, but East
can win the next club and play a heart to promote West's ◇Q. Rather than
aim for three spade ruffs, perhaps one could hope to find the ♣K onside,
in which case a lead up to the ♣Q produces a trick. As the cards lie, this
works no better. The queen falls victim to the king and once more a
trump promotion seals the contract's fate. Can either side improve on the
above? See page 92 for the second part of the solution.

HAND 15 SURPRISE RUN

```
                              ♠ A Q
                              ♡ A J 3
                              ◇ A 10 9 5 3
                              ♣ A 4 3
        ♠ J 10 8 4 3                           ♠ 9 6 5 2
        ♡ K 9 6 2          ┌─────────┐         ♡ Q 8 4
        ◇ J 7          W   │    N    │   E     ◇ K Q 6 4 2
        ♣ 7 2              │    S    │         ♣ 5
                          └─────────┘
```

W	N	E	S
		pass	3♣
pass	6♣	all pass	

```
                              ♠ K 7
                              ♡ 10 7 5
                              ◇ 8
                              ♣ K Q J 10 9 8 6
```

Contract: 6♣
Opening Lead: ♠J

HAND 16 PLAIN SQUASH

```
                              ♠ Q J 10 4
                              ♡ J 2
                              ◇ Q J
                              ♣ A 5 4 3 2
        ♠ 9 6                               ♠ 8 7 5 3 2
        ♡ Q 8 7 4          ┌─────────┐      ♡ 10 9 5
        ◇ A K 9 8 3    W   │    N    │   E  ◇ 5 4
        ♣ K 8              │    S    │      ♣ J 10 7
                          └─────────┘
```

W	N	E	S
1◇	pass	pass	1NT
pass	2♣	pass	3♡[1]
pass	3NT	all pass	

1.   15-16 with 4 hearts.

```
                              ♠ A K
                              ♡ A K 6 3
                              ◇ 10 7 6 2
                              ♣ Q 9 6
```

Contract: 3NT
Opening Lead: ◇A

HAND 15 SURPRISE RUN

Entries to the table may come in handy, so the ♠K wins the first trick. Declarer might now cash the ◇A, ruff a diamond, draw trumps ending in dummy and trump another diamond. West shows out at this point, which is bad news.

The heart suit offers various options: small to the jack would succeed against king-queen to any number, K-x or Q-x with West; low to (or leading) the ten deals with K-x or Q-x on the other side. All the same, nothing works as the cards lie. In second seat, West can cover the ♡10 or otherwise play low. Likewise, East follows low if the first heart lead comes from the North hand. Nor does any sort of squeeze or endplay bite. Discarding after dummy, East can easily defend the position.

Could another way of tackling the diamond suit alter the outcome? See page 93 for the second part of the solution.

HAND 16 PLAIN SQUASH

West cashes the ace of diamonds and, delighted to see the doubleton queen-jack on the table, continues with the king and nine. You can easily spare a club from dummy and, as it looks like an exit card might prove useful, you win the third round of diamonds with the ten. You know from the opening bid on your left that a lead up to the ♣Q stands little chance of bringing joy and duly consider other options.

As an inspection of the hand diagram reveals, West happens to hold a doubleton spade. It appears you can take advantage of this by cashing two rounds of spades and then playing a diamond. West can take two diamond tricks, on which you can throw two more clubs from dummy and a heart or a club from your hand, but then West seems to be in trouble. A lead away from either the queen of hearts or the king of clubs will give you your ninth trick.

Does West have any way to escape from the endplay? If so, can you still make the contract? See page 93 for the second part of the solution.

HAND 17 WRONG GAME

```
                          ♠ A Q 2
                          ♡ J 9 4
                          ◇ K 10 7 2
                          ♣ 8 7 5
        ♠ 7                                    ♠ 9 6 4
        ♡ A K 8 5          ┌─────────┐        ♡ 7 6 3 2
        ◇ 8 5 4        W   │    N    │   E    ◇ Q J 6 3
        ♣ Q J 10 9 3       │    S    │        ♣ K 4
                          └─────────┘
                          ♠ K J 10 8 5 3
                          ♡ Q 10
                          ◇ A 9
                          ♣ A 6 2
```

W	N	E	S
pass	pass	pass	1♠
dbl	redbl	pass	pass
2♣	2♠	pass	4♠
all pass			

Contract: 4♠
Opening Lead: ♡A

HAND 18 DELIGHTFUL DILEMMA

```
                          ♠ 9 8 3 2
                          ♡ A Q 4
                          ◇ A K 7
                          ♣ 8 7 3
        ♠ A Q J 10 5 4                         ♠ 6
        ♡ 5 2              ┌─────────┐        ♡ J 10 3
        ◇ 10 8 2       W   │    N    │   E    ◇ Q 9 6 5 3
        ♣ 9 2             │    S    │        ♣ K Q 10 6
                          └─────────┘
                          ♠ K 7
                          ♡ K 9 8 7 6
                          ◇ J 4
                          ♣ A J 5 4
```

W	N	E	S
			1♡
2♠	3♠¹	pass	4♡
all pass			

1. Value raise in hearts.

Contract: 4♡
Opening Lead: ♣9

HAND 17 WRONG GAME

The contract coasts home if West continues hearts, a club going on the ♡J. In practice, East's signal at Trick 1 warns against playing a second heart. The ♣Q switch comes and East must overtake with the king. If not, declarer can win, knock out the ♡K and again throw a club on a heart. It seems natural to allow the ♣K to hold and to win the second club; we take it from there.

If East has the ♡K, you can afford to play on hearts (no doubt after drawing trumps), but why would anyone lead the ace with no king behind it rather than a nice club sequence? Might West alone guard diamonds, with queen or jack to five or Q-J to any number? If so, running trumps would produce a squeeze. West's initial pass suggests this next question: Would pass West as dealer with ♡A-K-x-x, ♣Q-J-10-x-x and useful diamonds?

Do you think perhaps you could find a way to develop a diamond trick? See page 94 for the second part of the solution.

HAND 18 DELIGHTFUL DILEMMA

Suppose the first trick goes nine, small, queen, ace. What can declarer do from here? Cashing only the ♡A before leading a club allows East to hop up with the king and give West a ruff (there are other ways to defeat the contract). However, taking a second round with the ♡Q works little better. Then East gets in on the second (or third) round of clubs and plays a third round of trumps. Declarer wins in hand and has just losing options left.

If West holds the ♠A, as the bidding indicates, crossing to the ◇A and leading up to the ♠K will prove fruitless. Leading a low spade from the king is a much better play. If West grabs two spades and shifts to a diamond, declarer can ruff a spade and lead the last trump for a double squeeze: West protects spades and East clubs, leaving neither able to deal with the ◇7. West can, of course, prevent this by leading diamonds twice.

Can you improve on the above sequence of plays? See page 94 for the second part of the solution.

HAND 19 LETHAL COCKTAIL

```
                                ♠ J
                                ♡ Q 6
                                ◇ K Q 10 8 7 5 2
                                ♣ A 5 2
        ♠ K 10 2                              ♠ 9 7 6 4 3
        ♡ 8 5 3               ┌─────────┐     ♡ K J 10 7 2
        ◇ A 6 3              │    N    │     ◇ J
        ♣ K 9 7 3           │ W     E │     ♣ 8 4
                             │    S    │
                             └─────────┘
                                ♠ A Q 8 5
                                ♡ A 9 4
                                ◇ 9 4
                                ♣ Q J 10 6
```

W	N	E	S
	1◇	pass	1♠
pass	2◇	pass	3NT
all pass			

Contract: 3NT
Opening Lead: ♡5

HAND 20 ACE APPEASEMENT

```
                                ♠ 3
                                ♡ 10 6 5 3
                                ◇ Q 8 6 5 3
                                ♣ K 10 7
        ♠ J 6                                 ♠ A 10
        ♡ J 8 7 2             ┌─────────┐     ♡ K Q 9 4
        ◇ 9 4                │    N    │     ◇ A 10 7 2
        ♣ A 9 6 5 4          │ W     E │     ♣ Q 8 2
                             │    S    │
                             └─────────┘
                                ♠ K Q 9 8 7 5 4 2
                                ♡ A
                                ◇ K J
                                ♣ J 3
```

W	N	E	S
		1NT	4♠
all pass			

Contract: 4♠
Opening Lead: ◇9

HAND 19 LETHAL COCKTAIL

A lead away from the king must be more likely than one away from the jack-ten, so up goes the ♡Q, but the king covers this. A 4-4 heart break seems unlikely and so South witholds the ♡A.

East could clear the hearts but, with no entry, this would serve little purpose. Declarer can take the ♡A on the third round and drive out the ◇A. Returning a heart and, when this holds, trying a spade, does not help. At the point East switches to a spade, the ace goes up; the defenders score two hearts, a spade and a diamond. A club shift at Trick 3 looks better. South plays high and it is vital the ace stays in dummy. Fortunately, conceding a trick to the king leaves West on lead, who cannot gainfully attack spades. Declarer loses a club and two hearts but no spades.

East could try a spade at Trick 2, hoping for some tricks there. In essence, this needs West, who can have at most three spades, to turn up with A-K or A-Q. Can you beat the contract as the cards lie? See page 97 for the second part of the solution.

HAND 20 ACE APPEASEMENT

In case the ◇9 is a singleton, East may go up with the ◇A and return a diamond. If the play starts like this, declarer should drop the king and then overtake the jack with the queen. East may hop up with the ♠A on a trump lead from dummy and try a diamond. Declarer should ruff high, draw the missing trumps, and play a low club. Unaware of the guess, and to ensure success if South has an 8-2-2-1 shape, West will almost certainly grab the ♣A and the hand is over.

East does better to duck the first trick: South's known spade length makes it much more likely that the lead is a doubleton. Then if declarer leads out a high spade from hand, the defenders can easily arrange a trump promotion. They do not even need to cash their club winner before playing two rounds of diamonds.

Might playing a club at Trick 2 (in order to start trumps from dummy) succeed? See page 97 for the second part of the solution.

SECTION 2

More Testing

MINIATURE 1 OPTIMUM STRATEGY

◊ 2

◊ K Q 8 7 4 3

With this combined diamond holding, the declarer, South, needs to make four tricks from the suit in a notrump contract before the defenders get their long suit going. Fortunately, he has one entry to dummy, just enough stoppers in their suit, and adequate entries to the closed hand.

What layouts of the diamond suit would enable declarer to succeed in this objective? How would the situation change if the defenders fail to follow their optimum strategy?

See page 66 for the solution.

MINIATURE 2 SLIPPERY SPADES

♠ A K 8 6

♠ 10 3 2

Here you can see the spade holdings of South, declarer and North, dummy. Spades are not trumps.

Under what circumstances might it be possible for declarer to score four spade tricks? You may assume that there are ample entries to each hand and you can ignore the possibility that someone has been forced to discard from the suit. This time you may also assume that East-West will defend correctly.

See page 96 for the solution.

HAND 21 EXTRA VALUE

```
                                    ♠ J 10 6
                                    ♡ K J 5 2
                                    ◇ A K
                                    ♣ A K 10 3
           ♠ K 9 7 3 2        ┌─────────────┐      ♠ Q 8 4
           ♡ A 10 9 6         │      N      │      ♡ 8 7 3
           ◇ 8 4              │  W       E  │      ◇ 6 5 3
           ♣ Q 4              │      S      │      ♣ J 8 6 5
                             └─────────────┘
```

W	N	E	S
pass	1♣	pass	1◇
dbl	redbl	pass	pass
1♠	pass	pass	2◇
pass	2♡	pass	2NT
pass	3NT	all pass	

```
                                    ♠ A 5
                                    ♡ Q 4
                                    ◇ Q J 10 9 7 2
                                    ♣ 9 7 2
```

Contract: 3NT
Opening Lead: ♠3

HAND 22 JAILBREAK

```
                                    ♠ 7
                                    ♡ Q 7 6 3 2
                                    ◇ 9 2
                                    ♣ A K 9 8 3
           ♠ J 10 9 3        ┌─────────────┐      ♠ 8 6 5 4
           ♡ A 10 4          │      N      │      ♡ K 9 5
           ◇ A 8 7 3         │  W       E  │      ◇ K 10 5
           ♣ 7 4             │      S      │      ♣ 10 6 2
                             └─────────────┘
```

W	N	E	S
			1NT
pass	2◇[1]	pass	2♡
pass	3♣	pass	3NT
all pass			

1. Transfer.

```
                                    ♠ A K Q 2
                                    ♡ J 8
                                    ◇ Q J 6 4
                                    ♣ Q J 5
```

Contract: 3NT
Opening Lead: ♠J

HAND 21 EXTRA VALUE

Dummy plays the ten of spades and East faces a decision about whether to play the queen. Whilst ducking would work well if you had ♠K-x, going up with the queen caters better for your actual holding. It looks a close call, but for the sake of argument we assume East puts up the queen — else you have ten easy tricks and time to develop two more. When the queen appears, you must win or lose your second spade stopper.

You can unblock dummy's ace-king of diamonds, but how do you enjoy the rest of the suit? West will win if you lead a small heart to the queen, and duck if you try the king off dummy. Of course, either way you can proceed to drive out the ♡A, but West can continue with a low spade. Then when you give up a club, the spades run. Attacking clubs before hearts produces the same result: you lose three spades, a club and a heart.

Can you overcome the communication difficulties? See page 98 for the second part of the answer.

HAND 22 JAILBREAK

You clearly win the first trick. Shall we see what happens if you run five rounds of clubs? You can readily spare a diamond and a spade but both defenders retain three diamonds. A diamond now goes to the queen and ace, at which point West switches to hearts. The defenders cash their ace and king of those before throwing you in with a spade. East's ◇K-10 take the last two tricks.

It cannot help to play off your top spades before cashing the clubs. Then you must lose a spade as well as the two ace-kings. Nor will it help to attack hearts. With the ace and king divided, you will create a third heart loser if you do. If the ace and king of diamonds sit onside, you could lead the queen from hand and later play towards the jack. As the cards lie, this plan fails too.

To succeed you will surely need to play diamonds twice from dummy. Can you find a safe way to achieve this goal? See page 98 for the second part of the answer.

HAND 23 TERRIFIC TIMING

```
                              ♠ A K
                              ♡ K J 8 7 5
                              ◇ A 6 5 4
                              ♣ K 7
              ♠ 7 6 2                          ♠ 8 3
              ♡ A 10 3          ┌─────────┐    ♡ Q 9 6 4 2
              ◇ Q 9 8           │    N    │    ◇ J 3
              ♣ Q 10 9 4        │  W   E  │    ♣ A J 3 2
                                │    S    │
                                └─────────┘
                              ♠ Q J 10 9 5 4
                              ♡ —
                              ◇ K 10 7 2
                              ♣ 8 6 5
```

W	N	E	S
	1♡	pass	1♠
pass	2NT	pass	4♠
all pass			

Contract: 4♠

Opening Lead: ♣10

HAND 24 PROTECTING PARTNER

```
                              ♠ 5 3 2
                              ♡ K Q 6 2
                              ◇ A 8
                              ♣ A 6 5 3
              ♠ A Q 9 4                        ♠ J 8 7
              ♡ 4               ┌─────────┐    ♡ 9 7 3
              ◇ Q 9 3           │    N    │    ◇ J 7 6 5 4
              ♣ K Q 10 8 2      │  W   E  │    ♣ 9 4
                                │    S    │
                                └─────────┘
                              ♠ K 10 6
                              ♡ A J 10 8 5
                              ◇ K 10 2
                              ♣ J 7
```

W	N	E	S
			1♡
dbl	2NT[1]	pass	3♡
pass	4♡	all pass	

1. Value raise to at least 3♡.

Contract: 4♡

Opening Lead: ♣K

HAND 23 TERRIFIC TIMING

As North has shown a good hand, West might have underled the ♣A. However, as the cards lie, you cannot get a club trick and whoever wins Trick 1 will switch to a trump. With the ♣K gone, you cannot control who wins the second club, which rules out a club ruff. Even if the ♣K remains in dummy, you could only take a club ruff if someone (East most likely) holds the ♣A and a singleton trump. In that situation, neither defender can play a second round of trumps. This sounds something of a long shot, and hardly worth giving up the chance of finding the ♣A onside.

If the diamonds play without loss, you can afford to lose three clubs, but that would require someone to hold ◇Q-J doubleton. Might you do something with dummy's hearts to take care of the third club? See page 99 for the second part of the answer.

HAND 24 PROTECTING PARTNER

This hand revolves around declarer's plan to force a helpful return to set up the ♠K and the defenders' efforts to thwart this ambition. Suppose the ♣A captures the king and then comes two rounds of trumps. If West parts with a club, the contract makes. Declarer can eliminate the diamonds and exit with a club. The next club is ruffed, but then dummy wins the third round of trumps and the fourth club puts West back on play.

To survive, West should first release the ♠4 and, if the third trump comes before the diamond ruff, a diamond next. Then it is safe to throw the ♣2 after that. On the fourth round of trumps, West discards a spade, retaining a club with which to get off play (or cash).

Ducking Trick 1 looks better and West has to continue with the ♣Q or face an impossible discard after declarer ruffs out the diamonds and leads four rounds of trumps. After taking the ♣A, it must be right to ruff a club. Indeed this would pave the way to ensuring the contract on a 2-2 trump break. Does it succeed on the actual layout? See page 99 for the second part of the answer.

```
                    ♠ A 10 8 5
                    ♡ 9
                    ◇ K 10 6 5 4 2
                    ♣ 10 5
      ♠ 4                          ♠ K Q J 6 3
      ♡ J 10 6 5 3 2      N        ♡ A 8 4
      ◇ A J 8        W        E    ◇ Q 7 3
      ♣ 9 8 3             S        ♣ J 2
                    ♠ 9 7 2
                    ♡ K Q 7
                    ◇ 9
                    ♣ A K Q 7 6 4
```

W	N	E	S
			1♣
pass	1◇	1♠	2♣
2♡	3♣	all pass	

Contract: 3♣

Opening Lead: ♠4

```
                    ♠ A Q 6 3
                    ♡ A 5 3
                    ◇ 10 8 6
                    ♣ J 7 2
      ♠ —                          ♠ 10 8 4
      ♡ Q 7              N         ♡ K J 10 6 2
      ◇ K Q J 9 7 5 4  W      E    ◇ 2
      ♣ 10 9 4 3          S        ♣ K Q 8 5
                    ♠ K J 9 7 5 2
                    ♡ 9 8 4
                    ◇ A 3
                    ♣ A 6
```

W	N	E	S
			1♠
4◇	4♠	all pass	

Contract: 4♠

Opening Lead: ◇K

HAND 25 DISCARD DECISION

Declarer hops up with the ♠A in dummy to avoid losing a pair of spade ruffs. With the side entry to the ◇K gone, drawing trumps will surely fail, so at Trick 2 declarer plays a heart towards the king-queen. East steps in with the ace and cashed two spades.

West knows from the overcall that South will run out of spades after three rounds (it appears impossible to defeat the contract if only one spade will cash). This gives two defensive tricks and West hopes the red aces are two more, which means the trump suit must furnish the setting trick. It seems likely that East has a doubleton club, including one picture card, which is probably not the ace. If so, it will take a trump promotion to generate the vital winner.

Suppose West discards two hearts and East continues with a fourth round of spades. To stop the ♣8 from scoring on an overruff, declarer may ruff high, but two top trumps cannot pull the five still outstanding and the contract goes down. Is it possible to do better? See page 100 for the second part of the solution.

HAND 26 SENSITIVE STRIP

Looking at just the North-South cards one can spot nine easy tricks, but finding the tenth taxes the imagination. You have threats of sorts against East in hearts and clubs but a squeeze is still a long shot. By the time you have lost enough tricks to tighten the position your entries will surely have gone. For example, if you give up a diamond, receive a diamond return to ruff, duck a heart to East, and get a friendly trump back, you are okay. You can run the trumps for a criss-cross squeeze without the count. However, each defender gets the opportunity to break this up.

Elimination play looks like a better prospect even though tenaces appear to be scarce. West possesses exit cards in both minors and you must surely choose East as your victim. This player cannot afford to lead clubs twice, but that would be hard to arrange. Do you think declarer can find a way to obtain a ruff and discard? See page 101 for the second part of the solution.

HAND 27 RED HERRING

```
              ♠ A K 7
              ♡ A Q
              ◇ K Q 7 4
              ♣ A 9 7 3
   ♠ 6 2                        ♠ 10 5 4
   ♡ 10 8 7 4          N        ♡ K J 5 2
   ◇ 9 8 3 2      W        E    ◇ J 6 5
   ♣ K 8 6           S         ♣ J 10 4
              ♠ Q J 9 8 3
              ♡ 9 6 3
              ◇ A 10
              ♣ Q 5 2
```

W	N	E	S
	2NT¹	pass	3♡²
pass	4♣³	pass	4◇³
pass	4♡³	pass	4♠
pass	5◇³	pass	6♠
all pass			

1. 20-22 HCP.
2. Transfer.
3. Cuebid.

Contract: 6♠
Opening Lead: ♡4

HAND 28 OMAR'S DISCARD

```
              ♠ 8 5 3
              ♡ 9 6
              ◇ A K 6 4 2
              ♣ 8 6 4
   ♠ —                         ♠ K 10 9 7
   ♡ J 10 7 4         N        ♡ Q 8 5 3 2
   ◇ Q J 10 8     W        E    ◇ 7 5
   ♣ A K 7 3 2        S         ♣ 10 5
              ♠ A Q J 6 4 2
              ♡ A K
              ◇ 9 3
              ♣ Q J 9
```

W	N	E	S
1♣	pass	1♡	dbl
3♡¹	pass	pass	3♠
pass	4♠	all pass	

1. Weaker than raising via 2NT.

Contract: 4♠
Opening Lead: ♣A

HAND 27 RED HERRING

Since nobody doubled North's cuebid of 4♡, it seems natural to try dummy's ♡Q at Trick 1 but it loses to the king. On a passive heart return, you can make the contract with consummate ease if you could see that the ◇J sits onside and the trumps break 3-2. You can draw one round of trumps, finesse the ◇10 and ruff a heart high. You can then pull the rest of the trumps, unblock the ◇A and go across with the ♣A to discard your pair of club losers on the good diamonds.

East does better to switch to the ♣J. You could cover with the queen, knowing that the ace stands on guard if West produces the king. Assuming this happens, you continue by cashing the ♡A, playing a diamond to the ten, taking the ◇A and ruffing a heart. With the ♣A gone, you have to win the second round of trumps in dummy, hoping that whoever holds the missing trump must follow to four rounds of diamonds. As the cards lie, East ruffs the fourth diamond and the slam fails. Might you improve on this line? See page 102 for the second part of the solution.

HAND 28 OMAR'S DISCARD

This deal (or one very like it) arose in one of the big French tournaments, at Deauville or Juan-Les-Pins. At most tables, South declared 4♠ and the play proceeded in much the same way. Almost all the Wests cashed two top clubs and, on noticing their partner's echo with the ten and five, continued with a third round. The East players ruffed this and returned a heart, feeling a little aggrieved when it transpired that their partners had jump raised hearts on a jack-high suit. The declarers had little trouble using dummy's two diamond entries to finesse trumps twice. They lost the first three tricks but nothing else.

At one table, the famous Egyptian movie and bridge star, Omar Sharif, sat East. He and his partner recorded one of the few plus scores defending 4♠. Would you like to guess what happened? See page 103 for the second part of the solution.

HAND 29 ENLIST THE ENEMY

                        ♠ A K
                        ♡ 7 4 2
                        ◇ Q 9 3
                        ♣ A 7 6 4 2

    ♠ 7 3   ♠ 8 6 4
    ♡ K Q J 10 9 8   N   ♡ 6
    ◇ 10 5 4   W   E   ◇ A K J 8 2
    ♣ J 8   S   ♣ Q 10 9 3

                        ♠ Q J 10 9 5 2
                        ♡ A 5 3
                        ◇ 7 6
                        ♣ K 5

W	N	E	S
2♡	pass	pass	2♠
pass	4♠	all pass	

Contract: 4♠
Opening Lead: ♡K

HAND 30 MAJOR DEVELOPMENT

                        ♠ A 6 3
                        ♡ A Q 6 5 3
                        ◇ Q 8
                        ♣ J 10 9

    ♠ J 10 9 7 4   ♠ K 5
    ♡ 8 2   N   ♡ K J 9 7
    ◇ 9 7 4 2   W   E   ◇ 10 5 3
    ♣ A 7   S   ♣ K 6 4 3

                        ♠ Q 8 2
                        ♡ 10 4
                        ◇ A K J 6
                        ♣ Q 8 5 2

W	N	E	S
			1◇
pass	1♡	pass	1NT
pass	2♣¹	pass	2NT
pass	3NT	all pass	

1. Checkback asking for 3♡/4♠.

Contract: 3NT
Opening Lead: ♠J

HAND 29 ENLIST THE ENEMY

For fear of a heart ruff (and of a diamond switch), you waste little time before taking the ♡K with the ace. On the bidding, the chance of finding West with a doubleton heart and the ace-king of diamonds is zero, which dictates looking for another way to develop a trick.

Once you think about it, a 3-3 club split will not do you much good because the only route to dummy outside the club suit lies in trumps. With those 3-2, you can ruff the clubs good and draw two rounds of trumps but someone must be able to ruff the fourth round of clubs. If instead East holds four trumps, you can set up the clubs via a ruff, cross to dummy with a trump and lead a club, knowing you can overruff. However, having done that and gone back to the table, East still retains a trump to stop the clubs.

It looks like you need to find both top diamonds on your right since if West ever gains the lead you will lose two tricks in each red suit. Can you squeeze East down to three clubs and then exit with the third round of clubs to secure a diamond return? See page 103 for the second part of the solution.

HAND 30 MAJOR DEVELOPMENT

If the players' lead methods preclude West from having the ♠K, declarer may put up dummy's ace at Trick 1, trying to block the suit. If East hangs on to the king, this strategy succeeds. Playing on clubs then lands the contract. East may win and cash the ♠K, but there is no way from here to establish and run the spades. In fact, West does better to win the first club and shift to a heart, but any heart from dummy except the ♡Q deals with this. Low is correct as West might still possess the ♣K as an entry.

Once the ♠A goes up, East should unblock the king. After this, the defenders should prevail. East takes the first club and clears the spades whilst West still has the ♣A entry. Declarer certainly cannot improve on this by attacking hearts. Do you think that letting the opening lead run round to the ♠Q might provide a path to nine tricks? See page 104 for the second part of the solution.

HAND 31 PASSIVE POTENTIAL

```
                              ♠ K 10 9 8 5 2
                              ♡ A 7
                              ◊ 6 2
                              ♣ J 10 5
        ♠ 3                                      ♠ 6
        ♡ K Q J 8           ┌─────────┐          ♡ 10 6 5 4 3 2
        ◊ A Q 7 5       W   │    N    │   E      ◊ J 10 8
        ♣ K 8 6 2           │    S    │          ♣ Q 9 3
                            └─────────┘
```

W	N	E	S
			1♠
dbl	4♠	all pass	

```
                              ♠ A Q J 7 4
                              ♡ 9
                              ◊ K 9 4 3
                              ♣ A 7 4
```

Contract: 4♠
Opening Lead: ♡K

HAND 32 CANNED HEAT

```
                              ♠ 5
                              ♡ 6 5 2
                              ◊ A K 8 5 4 2
                              ♣ 8 4 2
        ♠ 8 2                                    ♠ K Q J 10 7 4
        ♡ Q 10 7 3         ┌─────────┐          ♡ J 8
        ◊ Q J 7        W   │    N    │   E      ◊ 10 9
        ♣ Q J 7 3          │    S    │          ♣ 9 6 5
                           └─────────┘
```

W	N	E	S
			1♣
pass	1◊	2♠	2NT
pass	3NT	all pass	

```
                              ♠ A 9 6 3
                              ♡ A K 9 4
                              ◊ 6 3
                              ♣ A K 10
```

Contract: 3NT
Opening Lead: ♠8

HAND 31 PASSIVE POTENTIAL

It takes no effort to put up the ♡A, ruff a heart and then draw trumps ending in dummy. To land the contract declarer requires two tricks from the minors. Does that sound too much to ask?

Suppose you try the ♣J at Trick 4. East correctly declines to cover and the king wins. A club comes back and you should play low from dummy to cater for ♣Q-x with East. If West holds K-Q of clubs, you can exit with a club after taking the ace; then you get a diamond round to your king or a ruff and discard. Alas, East wins the third round of clubs and switches to the ◇J. You put up the king, but West scores two diamonds to beat you.

You might decide to play a diamond to the king instead of attacking clubs. The ace captures your king and the defenders again succeed if they play a low diamond across to the ten and continue with a third round of diamonds. You will have to play clubs and, assuming East ducks the first lead off dummy, you lose two club tricks and the contract. Can you think of a better approach? See page 105 for the second part of the solution.

HAND 32 CANNED HEAT

Holding up the ♠A to exhaust West's spades is the obvious start to the play. East wins with the ten and continues with the king. Declarer may take the ace next round, or perhaps waits until the third round to make sure of the position.

The long diamond suit seems the place to look for tricks, but the lack of outside entries on the table presents a problem. All will be well if West puts up the queen or jack: one can duck. This preserves the link to dummy whilst keeping East off play. Of course, a competent defender will play low, meaning this line works only if you find West with exactly ◇Q-J-10 — hardly likely.

Other chances appear equally slim. For example, if West has ♡Q-J-10 alone, and East the ♣Q-J, it will be possible to make three hearts and three clubs without letting in the spades. What else is there? See page 106 for the second part of the solution.

HAND 33 DOUBLETON KING

	♠ A Q 5 2	
	♡ A	
	◇ K Q 9 6	
	♣ A 9 7 3	

♠ J 9 4		♠ K 10
♡ 9 7 5 3 2	N	♡ K 10 8 6
◇ 7 4 3	W E	◇ 8 5 2
♣ 10 6	S	♣ K Q J 2

	♠ 8 7 6 3
	♡ Q J 4
	◇ A J 10
	♣ 8 5 4

W	N	E	S
	1♣		pass
pass	dbl	pass	1♠
pass	3♠	pass	4♠
all pass			

Contract: 4♠

Opening Lead: ♣10

HAND 34 DIVIDE AND RULE

	♠ A K Q 10	
	♡ 8 2	
	◇ K 8 4 3	
	♣ 9 6 4	

♠ 8 2		♠ J
♡ A J 10 5 4 3	N	♡ Q 7 6
◇ 10 2	W E	◇ A 9 7 5
♣ K 10 7	S	♣ J 8 5 3 2

	♠ 9 7 6 5 4 3
	♡ K 9
	◇ Q J 6
	♣ A Q

W	N	E	S
2♡	dbl	3♡	4♠
all pass			

Contract: 4♠

Opening Lead: ♠2

HAND 33 DOUBLETON KING

Solution Part 1

On a non-club lead, the play would be straightforward. Declarer could afford to take the spade finesse, draw one more round of trumps and get rid of a club on the fourth diamond.

The ♣10 lead makes life more complicated. The presence of the ♣9 in dummy marks this as a doubleton (or possibly a singleton) and East's opening bid places the ♠K offside. This means that declarer must lose two spades and two clubs if the ♠K is doubly guarded. Consequently, for the contract to stand a chance, it needs a doubleton spade king. Despite this layout existing, simply playing ace and another trump results in failure. East cashes two clubs and continues with a fourth round of the suit, which allows West to overruff. Can declarer overcome this hurdle? See page 107 for the second part of the solution.

HAND 34 DIVIDE AND RULE

Solution Part 1

Suppose you draw trumps in two rounds and lead a diamond from dummy. Nobody wants to play the ace on a small card and the queen wins. You can go back to the table and play another diamond, but East ducks again. You try a third round of the suit, the ace wins this time and you find out about the 4-2 break.

If East returns a heart and you put up the king, you go down. The ace wins the first heart, the queen the second and a club switch leaves you reliant on the club finesse. You do better to play the ♡9, conceding two heart tricks and reckoning that a club round to the ace-queen or a ruff and discard will come next. You can also succeed if East plays a fourth round of diamonds, but you would need the inspired view of reading the ♣K as offside. You would cross to dummy with a trump and either play ace and another club or a heart to the nine depending on West's discard.

East should switch to a club after getting in with the ◇A. You will finesse the ♣Q, but the king wins and a club return leaves you one last chance, to find the ♡A onside, but it is not. Can you make 4♠? See page 107 for the second part of the solution.

HAND 35 HIDDEN ENTRY

                              ♠ A K
                              ♡ 9 5 4
                              ◇ 4 3 2
                              ♣ K J 8 6 3

    ♠ 9 6 2   ♠ Q 7 4 3
    ♡ A J 8 6 2   ♡ 10 3
    ◇ J 8 5   ◇ K 7
    ♣ A 2   ♣ 10 9 7 5 4

W	N	E	S
			1◇
1♡	2♣	pass	2NT
pass	3NT	all pass	

                              ♠ J 10 8 5
                              ♡ K Q 7
                              ◇ A Q 10 9 6
                              ♣ Q

Contract: 3NT
Opening Lead: ♡6

HAND 36 FATAL CHOICE

                              ♠ A 8 2
                              ♡ 10 7
                              ◇ Q 10 4
                              ♣ A 10 9 6 5

    ♠ 10 5 4   ♠ 9 6
    ♡ 9 8 6 5 2   ♡ 4 3
    ◇ 3   ◇ K J 9 8 7 6 2
    ♣ Q J 8 4   ♣ K 3

W	N	E	S
			1♠
pass	2♣	3◇	3♡
pass	3♠	pass	4◇¹
pass	4♠	pass	5♡¹
pass	6♠	all pass	

1. Cuebid.

                              ♠ K Q J 7 3
                              ♡ A K Q J
                              ◇ A 5
                              ♣ 7 2

Contract: 6♠
Opening Lead: ◇3

HAND 35 HIDDEN ENTRY

East puts up the ♡10 and it looks right for South to take this as the bidding places the leader with an entry. The obvious next move is to attack clubs and West must win the first round to prevent declarer from overtaking in dummy and switching to diamonds.

With the missing high heart marked with South, West might try a spade shift, but this is no good. After dummy wins the spade, two club tricks follow, on with declarer throws two spades, and West a spade and a heart. Then a diamond to the ten sets up the suit whilst keeping the danger hand off lead: two spades, one heart, four diamonds and two clubs are nine tricks.

East may elect to put up the ◊K in an attempt to gain the lead, but declarer can take that with the ace and return the ◊10. Since West holds the ◊J, this conserves an entry to the long diamonds whilst protecting the vulnerable heart holding.

Might West do better to clear the hearts after scoring the ♣A? See page 108 for the second part of the solution.

HAND 36 FATAL CHOICE

With the diamonds sitting wrong (as one would expect from the bidding), declarer cannot guess right at Trick 1, which means that the twelfth trick must come from elsewhere. Dummy contains a five-card club suit, but entries both to establish and run the suit present a problem. With the opening lead being a singleton, you could safely set them up by ducking the first round and ruffing the third if West has ♣K-Q-J precisely or plays high on the first round from K-Q-x. Even on that layout, you would require a 3-2 trump split so that you could draw trumps ending on the table. This all sounds rather unlikely.

A better bet is to play East, who has many diamonds, for a shortage in both majors. In that case, you might take two rounds of trumps, four rounds of hearts, and ruff a diamond in dummy. Are there any pitfalls in this plan? If so, can you overcome them? See page 109 for the second part of the solution.

HAND 37 EITHER WAY

```
                        ♠ Q 4
                        ♡ A 4 2
                        ◇ A 5 4 3
                        ♣ Q J 10 5
        ♠ A 9 2                      ♠ K 10 8 7
        ♡ Q J 7         ┌─────────┐  ♡ 10 9
        ◇ 9 8 6 2       │    N    │  ◇ K Q 7
        ♣ 9 7 4         │ W     E │  ♣ 8 6 3 2
                        │    S    │
                        └─────────┘
                        ♠ J 6 5 3
                        ♡ K 8 6 5 3
                        ◇ J 10
                        ♣ A K
```

W	N	E	S
	pass	pass	1♡
pass	2♣	pass	2NT
pass	3♡	pass	4♡
all pass			

Contract:　　4♡
Opening Lead:　◇8

HAND 38 SEVENTH HEAVEN

```
                        ♠ Q 9 4
                        ♡ A Q 3
                        ◇ Q J 10 6
                        ♣ K J 4
        ♠ K J 5 2                     ♠ 10 7
        ♡ K 4           ┌─────────┐   ♡ 8 7 5
        ◇ A 9 5         │    N    │   ◇ K 8 7 2
        ♣ 10 9 8 2      │ W     E │   ♣ A Q 6 3
                        │    S    │
                        └─────────┘
                        ♠ A 8 6 3
                        ♡ J 10 9 6 2
                        ◇ 4 3
                        ♣ 7 5
```

W	N	E	S
	1NT	pass	2♣
pass	2◇	pass	2♡[1]
all pass			

1. Weak, North may correct to 2♠
with longer spades.

Contract:　　2♡
Opening Lead:　♣10

HAND 37 EITHER WAY

Declarer faces two sure spade losers and a trump loser (and that depends on a 3-2 break), so cannot afford to lose a diamond trick. Dummy's club winners will permit two discards, which solves part of the problem, but one must also contend with the spade suit.

The opening lead, coupled with East's initial pass, makes it almost certain that the ace and king of spades are in opposite hands: West would hardly lead a diamond from a collection of low cards with an ace-king combination; East would surely open the bidding with ♠A-K and ◇K-Q. West might hold A-x or K-x in spades, but even then, entries will be a problem. Declarer really needs a spade ruff in dummy.

Going up with the ◇A, cashing two clubs and the top hearts before playing two more clubs works fine — if someone ruffs the fourth club. However, a smart defender will wait for the chance to draw two trumps for one. Can declarer find a way round this hurdle? See page 110 for the second part of the solution.

HAND 38 SEVENTH HEAVEN

The jack may as well cover the club ten, giving East the first trick with the queen. One option is to return a diamond so that West can continue clubs. Of course, as the bidding indicated, South has only four minor-suit cards. The defenders pick up the first four tricks, but then dummy's diamonds will deal with declarer's slow spade loser and the defense make just one further trick: the ♠K.

The ♠A guarantees an entry for the trump finesse, which means the ♡K cannot score. To have any hope the defenders will need a spade ruff, or at least to threaten one. If East leads the ♠10 at Trick 2, going up with the ace to draw trumps results in down one. The defenders can later play a club through the king and knock out dummy's ♠Q entry. Declarer can avoid this by ducking the first spade, but if the nine wins the next spade, it leaves the lead in the wrong hand. Can either side improve on this sequence? See page 110 for the second part of the solution.

HAND 39 POWERFUL POSITION

```
                          ♠ J 8 6 3
                          ♡ K 10 9 3
                          ◇ K Q J 8
                          ♣ 6
        ♠ A Q 2                            ♠ 5
        ♡ Q 7 6 2        ┌─────────┐       ♡ A J 8 5
        ◇ 5 4            │    N    │       ◇ 9 7 6 3 2
        ♣ K J 10 5       │ W     E │       ♣ Q 9 7
                         │    S    │
                         └─────────┘
                          ♠ K 10 9 7 4
                          ♡ 4
                          ◇ A 10
                          ♣ A 8 4 3 2
```

W	N	E	S
1♣	pass	1♡	1♠
2♡¹	3♡²	pass	4♠
all pass			

1. 4-card heart support.
2. Value spade raise.

Contract: 4♠
Opening Lead: ♡2

HAND 40 ENCHANTING ENDPLAYS

```
                          ♠ K J 9 2
                          ♡ K 9
                          ◇ 10 5 4
                          ♣ A 5 3 2
        ♠ 6                              ♠ 7 5 3
        ♡ Q 7 3 2       ┌─────────┐     ♡ 10 8 6 5 4
        ◇ 9 8 7 2       │    N    │     ◇ A K Q 6
        ♣ K 10 9 6      │ W     E │     ♣ 8
                        │    S    │
                        └─────────┘
                          ♠ A Q 10 8 4
                          ♡ A J
                          ◇ J 3
                          ♣ Q J 7 4
```

W	N	E	S
	pass	pass	1♠
pass	3♠	pass	4♠
all pass			

Contract: 4♠
Opening Lead: ◇8

HAND 39 POWERFUL POSITION

The bidding and opening lead tell East how to defend the first two tricks: capture the ♡9 with the jack but do not attempt to cash the ace. Although West called clubs, a switch to that suit serves little purpose. Declarer can go up with the ace and take two diamonds ending in hand before embarking on a crossruff. East cannot overruff the fourth round of clubs and West has no effective play on the fifth. In fact, winning the second diamond in dummy and ruffing hearts before clubs also succeeds. This reduces everyone to three cards and poor West has to ruff the third round of diamonds and then lead from the ace-queen of trumps. A diamond switch in the vague hope of a defensive ruff produces the same result. Again, declarer can choose how to time the crossruff.

Dummy's singleton club surely marks a trump shift at Trick 2. Can the contract survive if the defenders play three rounds of trumps? See page 111 for the second part of the solution.

HAND 40 ENCHANTING ENDPLAYS

East may try three high diamonds, but the third round fails to stand up. After ruffing, declarer can draw trumps and consider how best to tackle the club suit. With no information about the opposing hands, normal play is to cross to the ace, preparing to lead twice towards the queen-jack. This strategy succeeds on any 3-2 break, whenever East holds four or more clubs, and if East has the bare king. Today it would prove a mistake to tackle the clubs that way. A player who passes as dealer and turns up with the three top diamonds scarcely has room for the ♣K.

You could strip the hearts before lead the ♣Q for a finesse. If West fails to cover, you duck the second club and are home. Of course, a good defender will put the king on the queen (or jack). Now, whether you give up the first or second club, West can exit with the ♣10. Is there a better way to tackle the clubs? See page 112 for the second part of the solution.

HAND 41 SAVAGE SWITCH

```
                              ♠ 7
                              ♡ A J 9 2
                              ◇ K 4
                              ♣ A K J 6 5 2
        ♠ K Q 10 8 2                          ♠ A J 9 3
        ♡ K Q 7 3          ┌─────────┐        ♡ 10 8 5 4
        ◇ A 6             │    N    │        ◇ 7 3
        ♣ 9 4            │ W     E │        ♣ Q 10 3
                          │    S    │
                          └─────────┘
```

W	N	E	S
1♠	dbl	3♠	4◇
4♠	5♣	dbl	5◇
all pass			

```
                              ♠ 6 5 4
                              ♡ 6
                              ◇ Q J 10 9 8 5 2
                              ♣ 8 7
```

Contract: 5◇
Opening Lead: ♠K

HAND 42 SELFLESS DEVOTION

```
                              ♠ A J 10 9 8 7
                              ♡ 8
                              ◇ 9 5 4
                              ♣ A K Q
        ♠ 4                                    ♠ 6 5
        ♡ J 9 7 5          ┌─────────┐        ♡ A 10 6 4 2
        ◇ K 10 7 2         │    N    │        ◇ J 8 3
        ♣ 8 7 6 5         │ W     E │        ♣ 9 4 2
                          │    S    │
                          └─────────┘
```

W	N	E	S
			1NT
pass	2♡[1]	pass	3♠
pass	4NT	pass	5♠[2]
pass	6♠	all pass	

1. Transfer.
2. Two key cards plus the ♠Q.

```
                              ♠ K Q 3 2
                              ♡ K Q 3
                              ◇ A Q 6
                              ♣ J 10 3
```

Contract: 6♠
Opening Lead: ♣7

HAND 41 SAVAGE SWITCH

If you do not much care for the bidding, I am afraid that is how it went at the table. This deal occurred in a charity pairs played at many clubs across the UK. If I recall rightly, Marc Smith, who wrote the commentary, thought that a couple of us bid too much!

East might elect to overtake the ♠K with the ace, but for the sake of argument, we will assume the king holds. West could switch to the king of hearts, trying to knock out the entry to the long diamonds. This would succeed if, for example, South turns up with a 2-2-7-2 shape. As the cards lie, it permits declarer to get home via a crossruff, using heart ruffs as entries to trump spades on the table.

A club shift appears less attractive than a heart. South may well have just three cards in the rounded suits and, even if these comprise two clubs and one heart, dummy's ♣A-K and ♡A will take care of them. Again, a pair of spade ruffs would land the contract. The obvious way to cut out spade ruffs is to lead ace and another trump. Indeed this provides the only route to a plus if South's hand is a 2-2-8-1 shape. On the actual layout, declarer can counter by setting up the clubs and going back to dummy with the ♡A. Might West find a more damaging lead at Trick 2? See page 112 for the second part of the solution.

HAND 42 SELFLESS DEVOTION

Declarer could draw trumps and then take the diamond finesse, but this is poor play. It is much more sensible to play a heart from dummy before touching diamonds. If East has the ace and goes up with it — likely with the singleton visible on the table — the king-queen of hearts will provide two discards, removing any need to find the ♢K onside. If the ace fails to appear on the first round of hearts, it never scores, which should leave declarer nicely placed. Can you picture how the subsequent play might develop? See page 113 for the second part of the solution.

HAND 43 HEARTLESS RETORT

         ♠ 9 5 3
         ♡ A 9 3
         ◇ A K 9
         ♣ 9 7 3 2

West		East
♠ 7 4		♠ 8 6
♡ K J 8 7 6 5 2		♡ 10 4
◇ Q 6 3		◇ J 8 7 5 4
♣ 4		♣ A K J 10

         ♠ A K Q J 10 2
         ♡ Q
         ◇ 10 2
         ♣ Q 8 6 5

W	N	E	S
3♡	pass	pass	3♠
pass	4♠	all pass	

Contract: 4♠
Opening Lead: ♣4

HAND 44 BAD BREAK

         ♠ J 6 4
         ♡ 9 5 3
         ◇ Q 2
         ♣ A 10 8 6 2

West		East
♠ Q 8 2		♠ K 9 7
♡ —		♡ Q J 10 8
◇ K J 10 8 7 4 3		◇ A 9 6 5
♣ 9 7 4		♣ 5 3

         ♠ A 10 5 3
         ♡ A K 7 6 4 2
         ◇ —
         ♣ K Q J

W	N	E	S
3◇	pass	4◇	4♡
all pass			

Contract: 4♡
Opening Lead: ◇J

HAND 43 HEARTLESS RETORT

Suppose the play starts like this: ♣K, ♣A, ♣10 covered and ruffed, low diamond exit. Declarer could try the double diamond finesse, but there is a much better play. Put up the ◊A, pull trumps, take the ♡A and ruff a heart, freezing East out of the heart suit. Then finish the trumps, to reach this end position:

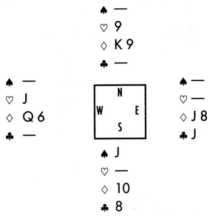

Now comes the ♠J. To keep the ♡J West discards the ◊6; the ♡9 goes from dummy and East surrenders. Can someone break up the double squeeze? See page 113 for the second part of the solution.

HAND 44 BAD BREAK

It seems natural to ruff the diamond and lay down the ♡A. West pitches a diamond and you may try running the clubs. However, even if East had three clubs, you would go down with the spades as they are. If you tackle spades early enough, you might pick up K-x or Q-x on your left or king-queen to any number on your right, but unfortunately none of these helpful layouts exist. Is there a way to ten tricks? See page 114 for the second part of the solution.

HAND 45 HELPFUL SPLIT?

```
                        ♠ K 8 6 2
                        ♡ A Q
                        ◇ 9 7 4
                        ♣ J 9 8 4
        ♠ Q                             ♠ A J 10 9 5 3
        ♡ 9                             ♡ 10 3 2
        ◇ Q J 8 6 2                     ◇ 10
        ♣ A K 10 7 5 2                  ♣ Q 6 3
                        ♠ 7 4
                        ♡ K J 8 7 6 5 4
                        ◇ A K 5 3
                        ♣ —
```

W	N	E	S
			1♡
2NT	pass	3♣	3♡
pass	4♡	all pass	

Contract: 4♡
Opening Lead: ♣A

HAND 46 TIMELY LOSS

```
                        ♠ 6 5 4
                        ♡ Q 8
                        ◇ 3 2
                        ♣ A K 8 6 4 2
        ♠ 9 7 2                         ♠ Q
        ♡ J 7 4                         ♡ A K 9 6 5 3
        ◇ A Q J 4                       ◇ 10 8 7 5
        ♣ Q J 5                         ♣ 9 7
                        ♠ A K J 10 8 3
                        ♡ 10 2
                        ◇ K 9 6
                        ♣ 10 3
```

W	N	E	S
		2♡	2♠
3♡	3♠	all pass	

Contract: 3♠
Opening Lead: ♡4

HAND 45 HELPFUL SPLIT?

Declarer ruffs the opening lead and must think how to reduce four losers (two in diamonds and two in spades) to three. The bidding rules out a 3-3 diamond split and makes finding the ♠A onside unlikely. Ruffing a diamond in dummy sounds like a nice idea, but doing that means cashing the ace-king of diamonds first. Simply leading them out will fail as East can surely ruff.

To protect the top diamonds it is necessary to lay down the ace first, cross to the ♡A and lead a diamond. This way, East cannot ruff a winning diamond and, after safely scoring the ◇K, declarer can give up the third round of diamonds. West can win but has no trumps left and is unable to prevent the ruff. Does the story end here or can the defenders thwart this plan? If they can, might declarer counter by adopting a different line? See page 115 for the second part of the solution.

HAND 46 TIMELY LOSS

The defenders can score the first four tricks with two tricks in each red suit. However, if they do so, they can pack up and go home. Remember the contract is 3♠. Declarer ruffs a diamond in dummy and, with the ♠Q bare, claims the balance.

East needs to trust West for either a doubleton club and a trump trick, or a club stopper, and spot that the ♠6 can hardly constitute a re-entry to the clubs. This makes a prompt switch to the ♠Q, to launch an attack on dummy's ruffing potential, a shrewd move.

On the bidding East cannot have the ◇A and the ace-king of hearts. This makes going across to play a diamond to the king rather pointless. When the first diamond comes from hand, West goes in with the jack to continue the assault on trumps. Declarer may try a second diamond at this point, but West wins to play a third round of trumps, leaving none in dummy. Three more round of trumps may follow. Can the defenders hold the end position? If they can, should declarer have done something different earlier? See page 116 for the second part of the solution.

♠ J 9 7 6 2
♡ Q J 9 7
◇ 5
♣ A K 10

♠ Q
♡ A K 6
◇ K J 9 4 3
♣ 9 7 5 2

♠ A K 10 8 4
♡ 4 2
◇ 10 7 6
♣ 8 6 4

♠ 5 3
♡ 10 8 5 3
◇ A Q 8 2
♣ Q J 3

W	N	E	S
1◇	dbl	1♠	2♡
all pass			

Contract: 2♡
Opening Lead: ♠Q

HAND 48 RIGHTFUL RUFFING

♠ A 3
♡ J 5 2
◇ K 9 6 3 2
♣ 7 4 2

♠ K J 5
♡ A 8 6
◇ Q J 5
♣ Q J 10 6

♠ 10 4
♡ K 10 9 7 3
◇ 10 8 7
♣ K 9 3

♠ Q 9 8 7 6 2
♡ Q 4
◇ A 4
♣ A 8 5

W	N	E	S
1♣	pass	1♡	1♠
dbl¹	rdbl²	2♡	2♠
all pass			

1. 3-card heart support.
2. A-x or K-x of spades.

Contract: 2♠
Opening Lead: ♣Q

HAND 47 ELUSIVE EXIT

East cannot gain by overtaking the spade to cash two tricks as doing so sets up dummy's jack. After the ♠Q holds, West could safely switch to a club. This presents little challenge. The ◇A and the ♣Q serve as entries to ruff two diamonds in dummy. West should instead play ace, king and a third trump. East does best to discard a club; after a spade pitch, North's fifth spade would end up a winner. With the spades likely to be 5-1 and the ◇K marked offside, declarer appears a trick short.

South's tenace position in diamonds suggests an endplay of some description. Cashing three rounds of clubs looks like the obvious next move to prepare for that. Can declarer oblige West to lead diamonds, allowing the queen (or maybe the eight to score)? See page 117 for the second part of the solution.

HAND 48 RIGHTFUL RUFFING

Another two-level contract, and this one may prove almost as much fun as the previous example. Declarer allows the ♣Q to win and captures the ♣K with the ace at Trick 2. Unless West holds both top hearts, which seems unlikely, the ♠K must sit over the queen. Moreover, having the top hearts divided rules out any prospect of a heart trick. Finding a doubleton king of spades sounds like one way to avoid a second trump loser, but more often the king will lie in the three-card holding. East's encouraging ♣9 at Trick 1 (and failure to overtake) suggests a 4-3 club division, perhaps giving West a 3-3-3-4 pattern. To avoid losing two tricks in each of the other three suits, dummy's diamonds must come into play. Declarer plays three rounds of the suit, noting the 3-3 break with pleasure. Having ruffed the third diamond, what is the best way to continue?

Crossing to the ♠A and playing a long diamond will bear little fruit. East, the short trump hand, will ruff the fourth diamond, still leaving declarer with six losers. Can you think of a possible improvement? If you can, will it suffice to land the contract? See page 117 for the second part of the solution.

HAND 49 GUESS AVOIDED

```
                        ♠ A Q 3
                        ♡ 9 6 3 2
                        ◇ A K 7
                        ♣ 7 5 3
        ♠ J 6 5                         ♠ 10 4
        ♡ A K 5              N          ♡ J 10 8 7 4
        ◇ 6 4 2          W     E        ◇ 8 5 3
        ♣ A Q J 9            S          ♣ 10 8 2
```

W	N	E	S
1NT	pass	2◇[1]	2♠
pass	4♠	all pass	

1. Transfer.

```
                        ♠ K 9 8 7 2
                        ♡ Q
                        ◇ Q J 10 9
                        ♣ K 6 4
```

Contract: 4♠
Opening Lead: ♡A

HAND 50 EASTERN ESCAPE

```
                        ♠ A Q 8 4
                        ♡ K 5
                        ◇ J 10 7 3 2
                        ♣ K 6
        ♠ —                           ♠ K 6
        ♡ Q 10 9 3 2        N         ♡ J 8 7 4
        ◇ A K Q 8 6     W     E       ◇ 9 5 4
        ♣ 9 7 5            S          ♣ A Q 10 2
```

W	N	E	S
1♡	dbl	2NT[1]	4♠
5◇	dbl	5♡	5♠
pass	pass	dbl	all pass

1. Raise to at least 3♡.

```
                        ♠ J 10 9 7 5 3 2
                        ♡ A 6
                        ◇ —
                        ♣ J 8 4 3
```

Contract: 5♠ doubled
Opening Lead: ◇A

HAND 49 GUESS AVOIDED

Perhaps you should have waited to bid 2♠ in the passout seat, and then North would not have put you to game. How can you make ten tricks when the bidding marks West with the ♣A?

One option is to play for ♡A-K-J tripleton (or for West to neglect to unblock with ♡A-K-x). In that case, you might draw three rounds of trumps, ruff a heart (if you have not already done so) and take the third round of diamonds in dummy. Finally, you pitch a club on the third heart, hoping West must win and open up the clubs. Another slender chance may come from finding West with ♣A-Q-J alone. To handle this you draw trumps, ruff two hearts and cash four diamonds before ducking a club.

Although you have more minor-suit cards than dummy, you can hardly ruff anything over there. Even if you could take two trumps and play four rounds of diamonds without running into a ruff, West will gain the lead twice in clubs, giving two chances to remove dummy's last trump; if it is East who holds the third trump, you will run into an overruff, which hardly helps. Can you find a line to make 4♠ as the cards lie? Better still, can you find one that does not depend on finding West with exactly a 3-3-3-4 shape? See page 118 for the second part of the solution.

HAND 50 EASTERN ESCAPE

Declarer ruffs the opening lead and plays a trump, West pitching a heart. Dummy's ace wins and a diamond ruff brings the lead back to the South hand. If the ♣A sits onside, playing a club to the king lands the contract, but East did promise values both with 2NT and the final double. It makes more sense to cash the ace and king of hearts and ruff a diamond. If, as seems quite likely, the suit splits 5-3, East has no more.

After stripping the diamonds, declarer exits with the second round of trumps, West throwing a club this time. After winning this with the king, East has a choice. Could the right one defeat the contract? See page 119 for the second part of the solution.

HAND 51 CANNON FODDER

```
                          ♠ 8 4
                          ♡ A 7 2
                          ◇ J 3 2
                          ♣ K 9 6 4 2
         ♠ 9 6                          ♠ 7 5 2
         ♡ K Q J 9 6 4      N           ♡ 5
         ◇ 10 9 5       W       E       ◇ A K Q 8 6
         ♣ 10 8             S           ♣ J 7 5 3
                          ♠ A K Q J 10 3
                          ♡ 10 8 3
                          ◇ 7 4
                          ♣ A Q
```

W	N	E	S
2♡	pass	pass	3♠
pass	4♠	all pass	

Contract: 4♠
Opening Lead: ♡K

HAND 52 BRILLIANT BATTLE

```
                          ♠ Q J
                          ♡ A 3
                          ◇ Q 4 2
                          ♣ A K 7 6 4 3
         ♠ 7 2                          ♠ 6 5 4
         ♡ K 8 7 6 4 2     N            ♡ Q J 10 5
         ◇ 9 5         W       E        ◇ A K J 10
         ♣ J 9 8            S           ♣ Q 5
                          ♠ A K 10 9 8 3
                          ♡ 9
                          ◇ 8 7 6 3
                          ♣ 10 2
```

W	N	E	S
	1♣	dbl	1♠
2♡	3♣	pass	3♠
pass	4♠	all pass	

Contract: 4♠
Opening Lead: ◇9

HAND 51 CANNON FODDER

Solution Part 1

Do you think North should have bid 3NT rather than put you to 4♠?
East would have known what to lead against 3NT!

   In a sense you can see ten tricks: six trumps, one heart and three clubs.
Alas, with the heart lead attacking dummy's entry and the club suit
blocked, you cannot readily cash them. If you duck the first trick in
attempt to conserve the ♡A, West can continue hearts, allowing East to
ruff the ace. Finding someone with the ♣J-10 doubleton would enable
you to draw trumps and overtake the second round of clubs. This sounds
like too much of long shot to consider if you can find a sensible alternative.

   Somehow, you need to exploit the 6-1 heart division and the stack of
diamond pictures in the East hand, which combine to wreck defensive
communications. Can you spot the way to do so? See page 120 for the
second part of the solution.

HAND 52 BRILLIANT BATTLE

Solution Part 1

If East cashes three diamonds, then ruffing the fourth round in dummy
is an easy route to the contract. A spade shift at Trick 2 prevents this, but
fails to save the day. Declarer pulls trumps, ruffs out the clubs and goes
back to the table with the ♡A. Killing the entry to the clubs must take
priority; East should lead the ♡Q at Trick 2.

   After winning the heart switch with dummy's ace, declarer might go
all out to set up a diamond ruff, but this proves a lost cause. East wins
both diamond tricks and can lead a trump each time. With dummy's ♡A
entry and trumps gone, declarer has little choice but to run the remaining
trumps. However, the defenders can withstand the pressure. West keeps
clubs guarded until the end whilst East protects the red suits. Is there any
way to come to ten tricks? See page 121 for the second part of the
solution.

BIG PENALTY 1

```
                        ♠ —
                        ♡ Q 6 4 3 2
                        ◇ 10 7 4 3
                        ♣ Q 6 5 2
        ♠ A Q 10 7 5                    ♠ K
        ♡ —                             ♡ 9 8 7
        ◇ K Q 6              N          ◇ A J 9 8 2
        ♣ A 9 8 7 4      W       E      ♣ K J 10 3
                            S
```

W	N	E	S
1♠	pass	2◇	2♡
3♣	4♡	6♣	6♡
pass	pass	dbl	all pass

```
                        ♠ J 9 8 6 4 3 2
                        ♡ A K J 10 5
                        ◇ 5
                        ♣ —
```

Contract: 6♡ doubled
Opening Lead: ◇K

BIG PENALTY 2

```
                        ♠ J 10 8
                        ♡ 10 7 5
                        ◇ J 9 5
                        ♣ J 10 9 4
        ♠ A 7 6                         ♠ Q 5 4 3
        ♡ A K Q 8 6 3        N          ♡ 2
        ◇ A 6 3          W       E      ◇ Q 7 4 2
        ♣ 2                 S          ♣ 8 7 6 3
```

W	N	E	S
			1NT
dbl[1]	all pass		

1. Penalties.

```
                        ♠ K 9 2
                        ♡ J 9 4
                        ◇ K 10 8
                        ♣ A K Q 5
```

Contract: 1NT dbled
Opening Lead: ♡A

BIG PENALTY 1

Seven tricks are easy, but at equal vulnerability an eighth trick would keep the penalty below the value of a small slam. North's poor trump spots, the 3-0 trump break, and the presumed 5-1 spade split make it hard work. Clearly, East overtakes the diamond with ace to return a trump and West throws a club. Declarer can win in hand, ruff one spade in dummy and ruff a minor-suit card. The obvious continuation of ruffing a second spade low fails. East can overruff and return a trump (indeed the trump return is not strictly necessary). Nor would it help to ruff the spade high since East will simply overruff next time. The solution is rather beautiful.

After one ruff, keep playing loser on loser in spades! West cannot continue spades or you would be able to set them up. Therefore each time West leads a minor, which you ruff in hand. You get to make all five trumps in hand and three on table – the spade ruff and then two tricks from Q-6-4 against East's 9-8. If after the third spade exit, i.e. the fourth round of the suit, West does return a spade, you must ruff high on the table, come to hand with your last trump and play a master spade.

BIG PENALTY 2

Many tournament players use a conventional double of a strong notrump to compete for the partscore rather than secure a penalty. Those who play for big money keep the double as natural — just for hands like this. Here, if you are playing for 10¢ a point and can find an ninth defensive trick, you could earn an extra $30 if they are vulnerable.

It looks obvious for West to run the entire heart suit and we assume that this happens. East makes five discards and with these should surely manage to communicate no preference between spades and diamonds. This will deter West from laying down an ace to look for encouragement. Therefore, West will exit passively with a club at Trick 7. Declarer starts with four club winners and the bidding makes it clear to play East for a queen rather than an ace. Does this provide a route to a fifth trick or are discards a problem? See page 122 for the second part of the solution.

SECTION 3

Tougher Still

MINIATURE 1 OPTIMUM STRATEGY

Solution (from page 30)

Clearly declarer can make four tricks if the suit breaks 3-3. It is also easy enough to do so if West has J-10, J-9 or 10-9 as the best play after small to the king fells the nine, ten or jack is to lead the queen next.

Declarer might also succeed if West has J-10-9-x because if both defenders follow low on the first round it costs nothing to duck the second to flush out a bare ace. However, West can thwart this by dropping the nine, ten or jack on the first round. Then it will look as though West holds the doubleton, in which case it is vital to continue by leading high.

Another possibility is that East has J-10, J-9 or 10-9. If West takes the king with the ace, declarer cannot go wrong, but a duck creates doubt. Now declarer will lead low, playing East for A-J, A-10 or A-9, which is more likely unless West always ducks from A-J-x-x, A-10-x-x and A-9-x-x

.

MINIATURE 3 BROKEN HEARTS

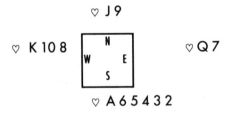

South is declarer in a contract of six hearts and this, unfortunately, is the trump suit. Maybe somebody forgot Roman Keycard Blackwood!

Under what circumstances is it possible to make the slam? You may assume that any necessary entries are available, that the rest of the hand is solid, and that the defenders will not err.

You may also wish to consider whether the same goal can be achieved when the opposing cards lie differently. See page 96 for the solution.

HAND 53 SURPRISE SOLUTION

```
                        ♠ A K Q
                        ♡ Q 9 5
                        ◊ 8 5 3
                        ♣ A K Q 8
        ♠ J 7 6 2                          ♠ —
        ♡ 10 3                             ♡ K J 8 7 6 4 2
        ◊ Q 10 7                           ◊ J 6
        ♣ 9 7 4 2                          ♣ J 10 5 3
                        ♠ 10 9 8 5 4 3
                        ♡ A
                        ◊ A K 9 4 2
                        ♣ 6
```

W	N	E	S
		3♡	3♠
pass	5♠[1]	pass	6♠
all pass			

1. Bid on with a heart control.

Contract: 6♠
Opening Lead: ♡10

HAND 54 SAFETY SUCCESS

```
                        ♠ A Q 7 6 2
                        ♡ K 7 2
                        ◊ 3
                        ♣ A 10 7 3
        ♠ J 9 8 4 3                        ♠ 10
        ♡ J 10 8 3                         ♡ 9 6 4
        ◊ Q J 4                            ◊ K 10 9 7 5 2
        ♣ Q                                ♣ K J 5
                        ♠ K 5
                        ♡ A Q 5
                        ◊ A 8 6
                        ♣ 9 8 6 4 2
```

W	N	E	S
	1♠	pass	2♣
pass	3♣	pass	3NT
all pass			

Contract: 3NT
Opening Lead: ♡J

HAND 53 SURPRISE SOLUTION

When dummy first appears, twelve tricks look routine, with just the third round of diamonds belonging to the defenders. The need to reassess comes quickly when East shows out on the trump lead at Trick 2. Suddenly one loser has become two. Finding someone (East most likely) with ♣J-10-9 alone would solve the problem, but this sounds a long shot.

Squeeze chances seem slim too. If West holds three diamonds and ♣J-10-9-x, there are the threats for a simple squeeze in the minors, but what about entries? After declarer unblocks the high spades, ruffs a heart to hand and gives up a spade, West will surely find the killing club switch. Likewise, giving East three diamonds creates the threats needed for a simple squeeze in the red suits, but again West upsets the timing by shifting to a club after getting in with the fourth trump. Can you visualize any way to make 6♠? See page 124 for the second part of the solution.

HAND 54 SAFETY SUCCESS

As a matter of routine, declarer wins the first heart with the ace, leaving a possible heart entry in each hand. Until you peek at the East-West cards, the contract seems almost assured. Having escaped an initial diamond lead, there is time to test both black suits. Declarer could attack clubs first, ideally by ducking a round. Whoever wins the club will surely switch to diamonds. It will then be possible to hold up the ◇A until the third round and make the contract in three situations: firstly, if clubs break 2-2; secondly, if spades divide 3-3; and thirdly if West's shape looks something like 4-5-3-1 (when you can afford to give up a spade).

Further analysis suggests that attacking spades offers better prospects. If they split 4-2, declarer can safely give up a spade no matter how the minors lie. If they are 5-1, somebody will show out on the second round, allowing time to turn to clubs. Is there even a way to make nine tricks when neither black suit breaks kindly? See page 125 for the second part of the solution.

HAND 55 STYLISH SEESAW

                                   ♠ K Q J 6 2
                                   ♡ 10 4
                                   ◇ 5 4
                                   ♣ A Q 7 3

        ♠ 9 8 4   ♠ A 10 7 3
        ♡ 8 7 2   ┌─────────┐   ♡ A J 9 3
        ◇ Q 10 8 2   W   │   N   │   E   ◇ K J 7
        ♣ 9 6 5   │   S   │   ♣ 8 4
                            └─────────┘

W	N	E	S
		1◇[1]	pass
pass	1♠	pass	2NT
pass	3NT	all pass	

1. 4+ diamonds or precisely 4-4-3-2.

                                   ♠ 5
                                   ♡ K Q 6 5
                                   ◇ A 9 6 3
                                   ♣ K J 10 2

Contract: 3NT
Opening Lead: ◇ 2

HAND 56 DOUBLE TAKE

                                   ♠ A K Q
                                   ♡ Q 9 5
                                   ◇ K 7 3
                                   ♣ A J 8 6

        ♠ J 9 6 2   ♠ —
        ♡ 10 3   ┌─────────┐   ♡ K J 8 7 6 4 2
        ◇ J 9   W   │   N   │   E   ◇ Q 8 6
        ♣ Q 9 5 4 2   │   S   │   ♣ 10 7 3
                            └─────────┘

W	N	E	S
		3♡	3♠
pass	5♠[1]	pass	6♠
all pass			

1. Bid on with a heart control.

                                   ♠ 10 8 7 5 4 3
                                   ♡ A
                                   ◇ A 10 5 4 2
                                   ♣ K

Contract: 6♠
Opening Lead: ♡ 10

HAND 55 STYLISH SEESAW

Solution Part I

Assuming the contract stands a chance of succeeding, declarer has a complete count of the hand at Trick 1. Since the major-suit aces represent certain losers, the only hope lies in restricting the defenders to two diamond tricks. This means you must place West with the four-card holding, giving East a 4-4-3-2 shape.

After ducking the first two diamonds, declarer takes the ◊ A on the third, pitching a spade from dummy, and plays a spade to the king. If the ace appears, life becomes a little easier. At this point, a return of either major in effect concedes an entry, and both the king and queen of hearts will score. A club return, which gives nothing away, proves more testing. Declarer can choose where to win this, but the obvious line is to run it to dummy and play a heart to the king. It would lose now to overtake the next club. Can you see why? Can you also work out whether nine tricks are on if East ducks the first spade? See page 126 for the second part of the solution.

HAND 56 DOUBLE TAKE

Solution Part I

This hand looks quite similar to hand 53, which means that it comes as no surprise when East shows out on the first round of trumps. On this spade layout, you definitely must lose a trick. Therefore, you have to find a way to escape a diamond loser. Catching someone with ◊ Q-J bare is one chance, albeit a remote one. Otherwise, you may need to come up with something special.

Since East holds three diamonds, you could easily arrange for West to give you a free finesse in clubs. You could cash the North-South top cards bar the ♣A, ruff a heart and exit with a trump. With nothing but clubs left, West would have to lead the suit, allowing dummy's jack to score. Alas, this third club winner leaves you a trick short. Yes, an endplay would suffice if you could make three fast diamond tricks (West might have a bare queen or jack), but not today. Can you bring home the slam in spite this? See page 127 for the second part of the solution.

HAND 57 SECOND NATURE

```
                        ♠ A Q 8
                        ♡ J 10 5 3
                        ◊ A J
                        ♣ A Q J 7
        ♠ 9 3                              ♠ K J 6 2
        ♡ K 9 8 6 4        ┌──────────┐    ♡ Q 7 2
        ◊ —             W  │    N     │ E  ◊ 8 6 4 2
        ♣ K 10 8 6 5 2     │    S     │    ♣ 9 3
                           └──────────┘
```

W	N	E	S
			1◊
2NT[1]	dbl	3♡	4◊
pass	6◊	all pass	

1. 5/5 or better in hearts and clubs.

```
                        ♠ 10 7 5 4
                        ♡ A
                        ◊ K Q 10 9 7 5 3
                        ♣ 4
```

Contract: 6◊
Opening Lead: ♠9

HAND 58 MOMENTARY MADNESS

```
                        ♠ K Q 6 5
                        ♡ Q 8
                        ◊ K
                        ♣ Q 9 7 5 4 3
        ♠ 8                              ♠ J 10 9 4 2
        ♡ 10 9 5 2        ┌──────────┐    ♡ J 6 3
        ◊ J 10 9 8 6   W  │    N     │ E  ◊ Q 4 3 2
        ♣ A 8 2           │    S     │    ♣ K
                          └──────────┘
```

W	N	E	S
			1NT
pass	2♣	pass	2♡
pass	3NT	all pass	

```
                        ♠ A 7 3
                        ♡ A K 7 4
                        ◊ A 7 5
                        ♣ J 10 6
```

Contract: 3NT
Opening Lead: ◊J

HAND 57 SECOND NATURE

Counting the clubs for two tricks, declarer appears a winner short for the slam. The bidding plus opening lead mark East with the ♠K and, although the club finesse figures to work, West will have the king well guarded. A squeeze of some sort looks the best chance and it seems second nature to duck the opening lead to rectify the count. East wins with the jack and, seeing too few spades to place West with a singleton, may switch to a heart up to the weakness in dummy. Declarer takes this with the ace, crosses to the ◇A, cashes the ♠A and ruffs a heart — it is vital to ruff the hearts to take the ♡Q out of the game. After this comes a trump to the jack, a second heart ruff, removing East's last card in the suit, and the rest of South's trumps.

At Trick 10 West must discard first from ♣K-x-x and the ♡K whilst the ♡J and ♣A-Q-J remain on the table. Throwing a heart allows the ♣J to go from dummy; a club finesse then leaves it high. Pitching a club works no better; in this case, the ♡J goes away and the ♣A-Q-J can all score. Clearly West can do nothing about the situation at this point. Could the defenders have broken up this simple squeeze in the rounded suits earlier in the hand? If so, can you find another route to twelve tricks? See page 128 for the second part of the solution.

HAND 58 MOMENTARY MADNESS

The king of diamonds wins the first trick and East encourages with the four. A club lead goes to the king and the ◇2 seems the obvious return. Declarer holds up the ace, throwing away clubs from dummy on both this trick and the next. To leave the diamonds ready to run, East plays the ◇Q on the third round of the suit. Now if a second round of clubs comes along, West can go straight in with the ace and cash enough diamond tricks to beat the contract. Has declarer a way round this problem? If you say yes, might the defenders find some other route to five tricks? See page 129 for the second part of the solution.

HAND 59 SOUTHERLY WIND

```
                          ♠ A K Q
                          ♡ J 7 6 3
                          ◇ Q J 7
                          ♣ A Q 10
        ♠ 8 6 3 2                          ♠ 10 7 4
        ♡ K Q 10 4        ┌──────────┐     ♡ 9 2
        ◇ 10 9 8 4        │    N     │     ◇ 6 3 2
        ♣ 7              W│        E │     ♣ 9 8 5 4 2
                          │    S     │
                          └──────────┘
```

W	N	E	S
			1NT
pass	6NT	all pass	

```
                          ♠ J 9 5
                          ♡ A 8 5
                          ◇ A K 5
                          ♣ K J 6 3
```

Contract: 6NT
Opening Lead: ◇10

HAND 60 KNOCKOUT MOVE

```
                          ♠ 10 8 6 2
                          ♡ J 10 8
                          ◇ A K 5
                          ♣ Q 7 3
        ♠ K J 9 7 4 3                      ♠ Q 5
        ♡ 5              ┌──────────┐      ♡ 7 6 3
        ◇ 9 4            │    N     │      ◇ Q J 10 6 3
        ♣ J 9 5 2      W│        E │      ♣ A K 8
                         │    S     │
                         └──────────┘
```

W	N	E	S
	1◇	1♡	
1♠	2◇[1]	pass	4♡
all pass			

1. Value raise.

```
                          ♠ A
                          ♡ A K Q 9 4 2
                          ◇ 8 7 2
                          ♣ 10 6 4
```

Contract: 4♡
Opening Lead: ◇9

HAND 59 SOUTHERLY WIND

Quite correctly, West has preferred a safe diamond lead to an aggressive heart. The North-South hands fit badly and, despite the presence of 35 high-card points, 6NT is a poor slam.

Ways that spring to mind for avoiding a heart loser include a bare king or queen with East and king-queen doubleton either side. Of course, both layouts sound unlikely. Placing West with the king-queen of hearts and aiming for an endplay sounds more attractive. If this defender has no more than three spades, three diamonds and four clubs, stripping the hand will prove simple. Declarer cashes winners from these three suits ending in hand and leads a low heart towards the jack. In practice West turns up with a singleton club, so probably holds a long card in one or both of the pointed suits. Unless this player discards down to three-card holdings, twelve tricks are not so easy. Can declarer succeed? See 130 for the second part of the solution.

HAND 60 KNOCKOUT MOVE

The bidding more or less rules out finding the ace-king of clubs in West's hand, which gives declarer three potential club losers. Since the odds are strongly against a doubleton ♣A-K, throwing East in with the third round of diamonds seems the best hope. Like on the previous deal, removing all possible exit cards will be straightforward if key suits lie well. Here this means a 2-2 trump split, as then a diamond return will allow declarer to ruff in dummy and throw a club from hand.

The pointed-suit aces win the first two tricks, and then comes a heart to dummy, a spade ruff and a second round of trumps. At this point, West shows out, making things awkward. Declarer can proceed to win in dummy and trump a second spade, but playing a diamond to the ace and exiting a diamond will fail. East can escape by playing a trump. Perhaps leaving ◊K-x on the table and running the trumps solves the problem. What do you think? See page 131 for the second part of the solution.

HAND 61 DIG DEEP

```
                        ♠ A K
                        ♡ A 6 5 3
                        ◇ 9 7 3
                        ♣ A J 7 3
        ♠ 7 2                          ♠ 8 6 5
        ♡ 10 8 7 2                     ♡ K J 9 4
        ◇ Q J 10 2                     ◇ A K
        ♣ 9 8 5                        ♣ Q 10 4 2
```

W	N	E	S
		1♣	2♠
pass	4♠	all pass	

```
                        ♠ Q J 10 9 4 3
                        ♡ Q
                        ◇ 8 6 5 4
                        ♣ K 6
```

Contract: 4♠
Opening Lead: ◇Q

HAND 62 MAGIC FORCE

```
                        ♠ A K 7 4
                        ♡ 10 9 2
                        ◇ A K Q
                        ♣ A Q 4
        ♠ Q 10 9 6 3                   ♠ 8
        ♡ K 3                          ♡ A J 8 7 6 5 4
        ◇ 3                            ◇ 9 7 4 2
        ♣ J 9 8 7 5                    ♣ 6
```

W	N	E	S
	3♡	pass	
pass	dbl	pass	4◇
pass	5◇	all pass	

```
                        ♠ J 5 2
                        ♡ Q
                        ◇ J 10 8 6 5
                        ♣ K 10 3 2
```

Contract: 5◇
Opening Lead: ♡K

HAND 61 DIG DEEP

Keen to avoid having the lead too often, East overtakes the ◇Q with the ace, cashes the king and exits with a trump. Even without this reverse order of play, declarer would deduce the diamond position. Good players rarely lead from Q-J-x in preference to their partner's suit. This means South's fourth diamond will not become a winner. Moreover, any attempt to ruff it in dummy will prove futile. If West held a singleton trump, East could ruff the third round of diamonds in order to play a second trump.

With only sixteen points missing and three already marked in the West hand, the club finesse seems doomed. Initially there is a slight chance of finding East with a 4-4-2-3 shape, in which case ruffing a club would set up the jack. Alas, that idea dies when West follows to two rounds of trumps. Now an endplay appears the best chance and East could hold ♣Q-10-9-8-x in a 3-3-2-5 shape. Then declarer could simply take two heart ruffs and draw trumps before playing the ♣K and a club to the seven. The actual layout is not so friendly. Can you make ten tricks as the cards lie? See page 132 for the second part of the solution.

HAND 62 MAGIC FORCE

West leads the ♡K and continues with the three, which forces declarer to ruff. A couple of rounds of diamonds then reveal the rather surprising split: the hand long in hearts holds trump length as well. Prospects appear somewhat bleak at this point. If East turns up with the ♠Q or the ♣J, it will come down in one or two rounds, and you will have a choice of ways to succeed. In that case you can surely afford to have a top card ruffed since a squeeze on West in the black suits will recover the winner lost. However, you hardly want to count on this possibility. Given the absence of a lead-directing double, East most likely has a small singleton in both clubs and spades. Can you find a way around that? See page 133 for the second part of the solution.

HAND 63 GREAT RECOVERY

```
                        ♠ K 10 3
                        ♡ J
                        ◇ Q 5
                        ♣ Q J 10 9 8 7 4
    ♠ Q J 7 6                         ♠ 8 5 4
    ♡ K 10 8 6 2      ┌─────────┐    ♡ 3
    ◇ K J 2          W │    N    │ E  ◇ 9 8 7 6 4 3
    ♣ 5               │    S    │    ♣ 6 3 2
                      └─────────┘
                        ♠ A 9 2
                        ♡ A Q 9 7 5 4
                        ◇ A 10
                        ♣ A K
```

South opens a strong artificial 2♣. East-West pass throughout.

Contract: 7♣
Opening Lead: ♣5

HAND 64 CLASH OF WILLS

```
                        ♠ A K 6 3
                        ♡ A K Q 10
                        ◇ 9 3
                        ♣ J 10 2
    ♠ 10 8 5 2                        ♠ Q 9 4
    ♡ 7              ┌─────────┐     ♡ J 6 5 4 3
    ◇ 8 7 4         W │    N    │ E   ◇ J 10 5 2
    ♣ A 8 7 4 3      │    S    │     ♣ 6
                     └─────────┘
                        ♠ J 7
                        ♡ 9 8 2
                        ◇ A K Q 6
                        ♣ K Q 9 5
```

W	N	E	S
			1NT
pass	2♣	pass	2◇
pass	6NT	all pass	

Contract: 6NT
Opening Lead: ◇7

HAND 63 GREAT RECOVERY

With just the North-South hands in view, 7♣ appears to be a very good contract. On a normal 4-2 heart break, it will be possible to ruff out the hearts and throw dummy's two pointed-suit losers on the long hearts. However, when declarer wins the opening club, cashes the ♡A, and ruffs a heart high, East discards a diamond. Suddenly prospects seem nowhere near as rosy. Even if you had enough entries to set up the hearts, they would provide only one discard. I suppose there is a slight chance of finding West with ♠Q-J doubleton. In this case, the ♠9 would be both a winner and the vital extra entry. As a glimpse at the full deal reveals, this long shot would fail. Playing in a grand slam allows you to dismiss any thoughts of an endplay. Could a squeeze really bring the two extra tricks required? If I said that this hand arose in a Scottish Cup match and that Hugh Kelsey was South, would you like to upgrade declarer's chances? See page 134 for the second part of the solution.

HAND 64 CLASH OF WILLS

Solution Part 1

You might play low from dummy, hoping that East misreads the position and puts up the ten. In practice we assume this would not happen and that the nine, ten and ace cover the seven. It must be right to play on clubs to knock out the ace and set up three tricks in the suit. The ♣J wins the first round of the suit and East discards the ♡3 on the second — interesting. If West takes the ♣A on the second round and continues with the ◊8, life is easy. You could start by winning the diamond and cashing two hearts to discover the bad break. You can work out from the way the diamonds have gone that either East began with four or the ◊J is dropping. In the former case, you have threats in each red suit, so taking dummy's two top spades and finishing the clubs will produce a simple squeeze. Either way one red suit will run. Can you still succeed if West holds up the ♣A more than once? See page 135 for the second part of the solution.

78 ● *Play or Defend?*

HAND 65 DELAYING TACTICS

                                    ♠ Q 6 4 2
                                    ♡ 6 5 3 2
                                    ◇ J 5
                                    ♣ 8 7 4

        ♠ K J 8 5   ♠ 9 7
        ♡ 10 4   ♡ 8
        ◇ 10 8 4   ◇ K Q 9 7 6 3 2
        ♣ A K J 6   ♣ 10 5 2

W	N	E	S
		3◇	dbl
4◇	pass	pass	4♡
all pass			

                                    ♠ A 10 3
                                    ♡ A K Q J 9 7
                                    ◇ A
                                    ♣ Q 9 3

                                    Contract: 4♡
                                    Opening Lead: ♣A

HAND 66 DRAWING TRUMPS!

                                    ♠ Q 9 4 2
                                    ♡ 8 7 3 2
                                    ◇ K
                                    ♣ A Q 10 2

        ♠ 10 3   ♠ A K J 8 7 6 5
        ♡ K J 10 5   ♡ 9 6
        ◇ J 8 6 5 4 3   W N/E/S   ◇ 10 9 7 2
        ♣ 9   ♣ —

W	N	E	S
		3♠	5♣
pass	6♣	all pass	

                                    ♠ —
                                    ♡ A Q 4
                                    ◇ A Q
                                    ♣ K J 8 7 6 5 4 3

                                    Contract: 6♣
                                    Opening Lead: ♠10

HAND 65 DELAYING TACTICS

East's signal on the first round of clubs warns West to switch at Trick 2. Diamonds seems the obvious suit to try. If East produces the ace, the defenders can probably cash out. Although South has the ◇A, attacking diamonds creates an exit card for West — a key factor as the cards lie. Having got in, declarer draws trumps in two rounds and must think how to avoid losing three clubs as well as a spade. A chance, albeit a slim one, is to play East for a bare ♠K. Then running the trumps will extract West's diamonds and giving up the third spade will result in a lead away from the ♣K.

Clearly, there is little hope if East holds a guarded ♠K as that card will provide an entry for leading through the ♣Q. Luckily, as it looks like East has ten cards in the minors, West figures to hold the ♠K. In the unlikely event that spades split 3-3 and West hops up with the king on a low card, you can make three spade tricks and the contract. Can you spot a more realistic chance? See page 136 for the second part of the solution.

HAND 66 DRAWING TRUMPS!

The chance that the heart finesse will work for declarer appears very slim: ace-king-jack to seven spades and a king (and a void) on the side sounds far too good for a weak 3♠ opening, even when vulnerable. Nor does a doubleton ♡K seem likely: for one thing many people would not preempt with four cards in the other major; for another there is simply far more room for hearts in the hand with fewer spades. Until West follows to a round of trumps, finding East with a 7-1-4-1 shape probably represents declarer's best hope. There is even a choice of endplays: either strip the pointed suits and duck a heart, or cash the ♡A and the two diamonds before giving East the fourth round of spades. The former option also caters for precisely ♡K-J-10 or ♡K-J-10-9 with West, so it remains as something to consider. Still, it would not work today. Can any line bring home the slam? See page 137 for the second part of the solution.

HAND 67 GUARDED PROGNOSIS

```
              ♠ K 8 3
              ♡ 9 7 2
              ◇ 6 4 3
              ♣ 8 7 4 3
♠ J 6                        ♠ Q 9 7 4 2
♡ J 10 8 5 3                 ♡ A Q 6 4
◇ K Q J 10 5                 ◇ 8 7 2
♣ 6                          ♣ Q
              ♠ A 10 5
              ♡ K
              ◇ A 9
              ♣ A K J 10 9 5 2
```

W	N	E	S
		pass	1♣
2NT[1]	pass	4♡	5♣
all pass			

1. At least 5-5 in the reds.

Contract: 5♣
Opening Lead: ◇K

HAND 68 MAGNIFICENT RESISTANCE

```
              ♠ K J 10 6
              ♡ A J 2
              ◇ Q 7 5
              ♣ A Q 10
♠ 2                          ♠ 4
♡ Q 9 7 5 4                  ♡ K 10 6
◇ 10 8 6 3                   ◇ A K J 2
♣ 8 7 3                      ♣ K J 9 5 4
              ♠ A Q 9 8 7 5 3
              ♡ 8 3
              ◇ 9 4
              ♣ 6 2
```

W	N	E	S
		1♣	3♠
pass	4♠	all pass	

Contract: 4♠
Opening Lead: ♣7

From declarer's viewpoint, it seems right to duck the first trick. This cuts the defensive communications whilst tightening the end position. Doing so involves negligible risk because if the diamonds were 7-1, surely somebody would have gone on to 5♡. If West continues diamonds, the ace wins and cashing the ♣A draws trumps. The problem remains of how to avoid losing a spade.

West might hold ♠Q-J doubleton or maybe one of these cards as a singleton, but neither situation seems very likely. A practical shot would be to play East for the ♡A and ♠Q-J and aim for a throw in. Running the trumps will reduce everyone to four cards, and you can expect to exit with a heart to East's bare ace. To get a better count of the hand you might use dummy's ♣8 as an entry to ruff a diamond, but it would blow the contract as the cards lie. Observe the effect of simply running trumps:

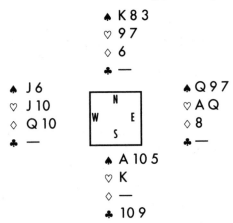

```
                ♠ K 8 3
                ♡ 9 7
                ◇ 6
                ♣ —
  ♠ J 6                        ♠ Q 9 7
  ♡ J 10          N            ♡ A Q
  ◇ Q 10      W       E        ◇ 8
  ♣ —             S            ♣ —
                ♠ A 10 5
                ♡ K
                ◇ —
                ♣ 10 9
```

On the penultimate trump, West can spare a diamond and North a low spade, but East feels the pitch. A spade discard is out for sure, which just leaves the red suits. If East releases the ♡Q, West must throw a diamond on the next club; letting a spade go would create a finesse position whilst parting with a heart would enable declarer to set up a heart trick. Once West has no diamonds, a heart goes from dummy and East surrenders. Any discard would cost a trick.

In practice, East will probably throw a diamond on the next to last trump, trusting West to look after the suit. In this case, again the guard menace in spades dictates West's final discard: it has to be a heart. Now dummy's ◇6 becomes redundant whilst poor East comes under further pressure. A spade discard is instantly fatal whilst a heart pitch enables declarer to set up a heart.

If East started with the queen and jack of spades, would the same basic strategy work? Then West would be able to keep a diamond, two hearts and a spade in the four-card ending. At Trick 10, declarer would exit with a heart to the now bare ace and East would need to lead high to create a guess. However, many a defender would play for the legitimate chance of ♠A-9-x with South and lead a low spade. In any event, if you find out who holds the queen and jack of hearts, East's initial pass may provide a clue about the spade position: a fair number of players open on hands with 5-4 in the majors at the slightest excuse.

Returning to the deal as it stands, can the defenders do any better? See page 138 for the second part of the solution.

HAND 68 MAGNIFICENT RESISTANCE

Solution Part I

It seems clear for declarer to finesse dummy's ♣10 at Trick 1 and the jack wins. Since the title has probably given away that there is a way to defeat the contract, let us consider the position from East's point of view. To jump to 3♠ South very probably holds a seven-card spade suit, almost certainly headed by the ace. These winners plus the two aces on the table add up to nine. This means that if any of the ♣Q, ◇Q or ♡J takes a trick, the contract will succeed. For the present, you face an awkward choice about what to return. If you cash the ace and king of diamonds, you set up dummy's queen, but if you fail to do so you surely risk being thrown in later. Although you could have an opening bid without the club king, you cannot seriously expect declarer to finesse in clubs. Whilst the lead of the ♣7 could have come from K-9-7 or K-8-7, the truth is that this card merely increases the chance that you hold the ♣K.

Suppose you decide on a passive trump return. Shall we see what happens? Placing you with most of the missing values, declarer produces an avalanche of trumps. You find two club discards painless enough and you can easily spare one small heart. You can also afford to part with the ◇J (keeping your options open for later) and, once a heart has gone from dummy, a second heart. This brings us to here with South on lead:

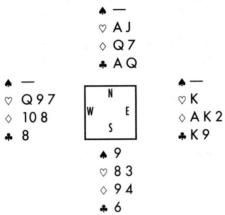

```
              ♠ —
              ♡ A J
              ◇ Q 7
              ♣ A Q
♠ —                        ♠ —
♡ Q 9 7      N             ♡ K
◇ 10 8    W     E          ◇ A K 2
♣ 8          S             ♣ K 9
              ♠ 9
              ♡ 8 3
              ◇ 9 4
              ♣ 6
```

On the ♠9, West discards a low heart and dummy the jack. What can you do? If you throw another club, a club lead to the ace can fell your king. If, as shown in the diagram, West has thrown the ♣3 and hung on to the ♣8, baring the ♣K probably offers your best chance: after all, you could have started with a 1-3-3-6 shape. In practice, partner may well have discarded the ♣8, trying to help you, in which case declarer will guess right.

If you part with the ◇2 on the last spade, a heart to the ace and a diamond exit follows. You make two diamonds but must then lead into the club tenace. You could avoid that happening by throwing the ◇A, but a different fate lies in store. Declarer takes dummy's rounded suit aces and puts you in with a club; the ◇Q then scores at the end. Finally, you can postpone the evil moment by throwing the ♡K. In that case crossing to the ♡A squeezes you out of a diamond, with the same options as if you had thrown one on the round before. How can you prevent this? See page 139 for the second part of the solution.

SECTION 4
Solutions for 'Fairly Easy'

HAND 1 DIRECT ACTION

You can make 3NT. Assuming that few players would lead low from a spade suit headed by the K-J-10, the solution is really quite simple, using a little-known blocking play.

Put up the ace of spades at Trick 1. Since West alone can gain the lead in diamonds, if East drops the ten, your queen and nine guarantee you a second stopper. In practice, East follows low.

You run the jack of diamonds to the queen and West may continue with a low spade. If that happens, you allow the ten to hold. You win the likely club switch and continue diamonds, knocking out the ace. The suit is now set up and you still have spades stopped. You only score one spade trick, but you can live with that. Three diamonds, one spade, three hearts and two clubs add up to nine.

If West prefers to cash the king of spades at Trick 3, this fells East's ten. Again, your queen and nine provide a double stopper and the contract is safe.

HAND 2 ACHILLES' HEEL

East can defeat 3NT by switching to exactly the right card.

A low heart does not work because the nine scores. The defenders lack the time to make both a heart and a second spade trick. A switch to the king of hearts fares even worse as this slows the potential defensive heart winner and gives declarer three tricks with no effort.

The ten of hearts is the killer. If declarer wins this in dummy, West plays the seven or eight and East wins the first diamond to continue with the ♡4. A further unblock in hearts leaves the king-six as a tenace over dummy, which then yields two tricks after West gets in with the diamond ace. These, together with two diamonds and a spade are enough.

If declarer goes up with ace at Trick 2, East still wins the first diamond and this time has the luxury of deciding whether or not to cash the ♡K before reverting to spades. The defenders make two spades, one heart and two diamonds.

HAND 3 TENS AND NINES

You can make the notrump game and to do so you indeed need to start diamonds from dummy. You should cross over with a club, ideally at Trick 2 (cashing the king first could cost if East, who has the long clubs, held a late diamond entry). Then lead the ◇ 10, intending to run it. West can do no better than to win and shift to a heart. After the nine falls to the ten, you hold up your ace until the third round. Whatever the defenders do now, you can easily cash the ace of diamonds to drop the queen and lead towards dummy's two pointed-suit tens.

If East covers the ten of diamonds with the queen, you win with the ace and play twice towards the nine of diamonds — it all comes to the same thing.

With the ten of spades and the ten-nine of diamonds playing such a crucial role, North's raise to 3NT on a 3-3-4-3 nine count now appears fully justified.

HAND 4 ENTRY EFFICIENCY

West can prevent the ♠6 from becoming an entry by flying in with the eight on the first round of spades. Somehow, you will need to manage with a single entry. Therefore, whatever you do first must open up the possibility of leading from dummy again.

It is no good playing East for K-x or Q-x of clubs. If you lead small to the jack, West simply ducks. No, you require both the king and queen of clubs on your right — quite possible given the bidding. In order to take advantage of this situation you need to attack clubs from hand. After perhaps first cashing the ♠A, you should play the jack of clubs. East can win and exit with a spade (or a heart), but on reaching dummy you lead the ♣10. If East covers, the ♣9 provides a re-entry. If the ♣10 holds, you remain on the table to play diamonds at once.

HAND 5 BATH TIME BLUES

If East had the ace of hearts, a shift to the ♡4 would succeed, but we have established that this fails as the cards lie. Precisely one card will do the trick here: the queen of hearts.

If the ace captures the queen, the defenders can later run three heart tricks. East will get in with the ◇A, cash the king of hearts and then the ten-seven form a tenace over the eight. Three hearts, a diamond and a spade are enough for a set.

If the queen of hearts wins, West continues with the three to East's king. Playing the ace at this point produces the same result as taking it on the previous trick, so declarer ducks. Once this happens, East abandons hearts and reverts to spades. Now declarer has to play the jack to escape for one off.

HAND 6 PASS THE PARCEL

East's double coupled with West's lead confirm the 2-5 club break (you have no problem if they split 1-6 as anyone with six decent clubs, who passed as dealer, cannot hold two diamond entries). You will need to try something different in clubs, but putting up the ace in dummy does not provide the answer. This leaves West with a second club to lead after getting in with the ◇K.

To make 3NT you need to duck the opening lead completely. West continues clubs and you must cover this with dummy's ten, retaining a double stopper. Seeing no future in clubs, East may shift to a spade after taking the second trick. You can deal with this by playing the ace on the jack or letting a low spade run round to dummy. Either way you avoid losing a spade trick, which will also be the case if East switches to a passive heart. Although you score only one club, you make game with two spades (at least), three hearts, three diamonds and a club.

Yes, another time you might go down this way when a near novice would make the contract. If East has cunningly led the jack of spades from Q-J-x and West holds both diamond entries, you will lose two clubs, two diamonds and a spade. If this does happen, you can count yourself unlucky and congratulate your right-hand opponent.

HAND 7 TEN•TON TRUCK

If you can draw trumps, you can enjoy the diamonds and discard any remaining losers on them. A 3-3 break is against the odds and you can cater for a 4-2 split if you tackle the trump suit in the right way. However, if you lead small to the ten, you go down. East wins with the jack and switches to a small heart. After the defenders cash the ace and king of hearts, they play a third round for West to ruff. Dummy's lowly ♠2 proves useless.

With that line you were almost there. Run the seven on the first round of trumps. Now the ♠10 stands ready to deal with the third round of hearts. Yes, you risk going down if West has jack to four trumps (and no nine), but anyone who ducks smoothly with that deserves to beat the contract. This line would also backfire if someone (probably East) has five spades and four diamonds (when you miss taking quick discards). There is also a vague chance that East might turn up with ♠J-9-x and ♡A-x or ♡K-x and score an overruff. These dangers seem even more unlikely.

HAND 8 ACHIEVING ACCESS

Tackling hearts carries an attraction because dummy's pips are good enough for you to force an entry. You can then pitch some losers on the king-queen of clubs and take the spade finesse. The snag is you need to use both good clubs to shed diamonds, which quite likely leaves you with a third-round spade loser.

Perhaps you try a low spade to the queen at Trick 4. No, East wins with the king and has various ways to exit safely. Instead you should lead the jack of spades, trying to lure the king. If the move works, you take the spade return in hand, cross to the ♠Q and play a trump (or you can take two diamond discards first). East can rise with the ♡A but cannot help either putting you back on the table or exiting with a friendly trump. It comes to much the same thing if the ♠J holds at Trick 4 (or if you preceded the ♠J with the ♠A, which proves equally effective). After the ♠J wins, you continue with ace and another spade. East wins with the king and must play a rounded suit, thereby giving you the entries required to finesse trumps twice.

HAND 9 DELICATE DIAMONDS

After a low diamond comes from dummy, East should stick in the nine. The king must take this, or declarer has no stopper in the suit at all. Then East gets in with ♣A as before, but this time the queen takes the second diamond and the suit will run. Does this mean should the contract always go down?

Norwegian star, Geir Helgemo, knew exactly what to do with this combination. When he saw it, he put up the jack from dummy, leaving his opponents with no way to unscramble the diamonds. Whether East wins or ducks, West's queen and ten combine to block the suit. Neither would taking the ace and switching to a spade help. The ace captures West's jack and the defenders make only two spades plus a couple of aces.

Yes, the ◇10 opening lead would break the contract, as would the ♠3. Both actions seem rather far-fetched.

HAND 10 NULLIFYING NORTH

Like it or not, you really need to place South with an eight-card spade suit. This seems to make life rather difficult. Indeed, you cannot do much about an 8-1-2-2 shape. Declarer has nine certain tricks and you cannot counter the threats of a diamond ruff and of a second heart trick. Therefore, you mentally assume an 8-0-3-2 pattern for South, although at first sight the problems seem to remain the same. If you switch to trumps, North's ten provides an entry for cashing two heart winners. If you fail to do so, a diamond ruff provides access to dummy.

To succeed you have to go back one trick. West knows just as well as East whether a third club will stand up. At Trick 2, you should return a low club. A trump attack from the left side of the table proves rather more effective. If the ten goes up, the king covers it, forcing declarer to win the trick in hand. Otherwise, you can duck to produce the same result. Either way, declarer can do no better than to try a diamond to the king and ace. A second trump lead then leaves dummy not taking a single trick.

Note that the club underlead also defeats the 7-1-2-3 hand without the ♠J we discussed earlier. Then West, looking at J-x of trumps and a singleton heart, switches to a heart at Trick 3.

HAND 11 USEFUL CONCESSION

With the hearts dividing evenly, you can establish a long heart without creating extra losers along the way. However, barring an unusual layout of the red suits, the defenders will have time to get the diamonds going before you can enjoy the good heart.

You need to develop the club suit, and you must concede a club at a point when a spade stopper remains in dummy. After cashing the ♠Q at Trick 2, you simply duck a club. You can win the likely diamond return (nothing else causes trouble) and play a club to the ace. West shows out, which enables you to follow the ace-king of spades with the marked club finesse. Since the odds are against scoring five club tricks when you would require a 3-2 break and a successful finesse, ducking the first round of the suit would probably still be right at pairs scoring.

HAND 12 ANGLE OF ATTACK

Suppose East shifts to the two of clubs at Trick 2. Dummy's ace captures the king and now declarer can even afford to come over with a diamond to start trumps from hand. If East wins with the queen and plays the queen of clubs, this sets up dummy's suit. Playing the ten of clubs works no better. Once the weak hand turns up with the club king, the opening bidder surely has the queen. South discards on the present trick and can only be made to ruff once.

To defeat the contract you must switch to the queen of clubs. You can go in with the ♠Q on the first round of trumps and continue clubs. Assuming South ruffs, West hangs on to the king, which means that you can play a second club with deadly effect when you get in with ♠A. Declarer cannot counter even by taking the inspired view to abandon trumps. The spade seven proves just good enough to frustrate an attempt to cash three diamonds, pitch one on the ♡Q, and ruff two in dummy.

HAND 13 SAFE FINESSING

If East can take the first round of spades with the ten, a switch to a low heart proves a killer. You cannot let the ♡10 win, or West can play a spade to the ace. Having taken it, any subsequent heart lead will present you with only losing options: win in dummy and lose two hearts, or duck and see East go back to spades. In either case, three losers in the majors and two in diamonds spell defeat.

You can make this contract. To do so you must call for the ♠A straight away. Then take one diamond finesse, win the club or heart shift on the table and take a second diamond finesse (even though East shows out). West makes another diamond trick, but you still have all suits stopped.

Note that you risk nothing in putting up dummy's ♠A. Since both the diamond finesses go into the hand on your left, you still have a double stopper, which would be important if the lead was from king to four. You are surely going down if West started with king to five or six spades and the king-jack of diamonds — with no side entry, you can hardly play your ◊A on the second round of diamonds whether East follows or not.

HAND 14 CONQUERING QUEENS

You can make 5◊ on a trump switch. Follow the black aces with spade ruffs and exit from dummy with the ♣Q. East wins and can neither draw dummy's last trump nor play a heart to much effect. Declarer ruffs the heart, takes a third spade ruff, and ruffs a club. The ◊A drops the queen, leaving South's remaining cards high.

A slight change to the above timing proves equally effective: lead the ♣Q and duck after taking just one spade ruff. Even so, the contract should fail. East needs to foresee this avoidance play in clubs and concentrate on promoting West's ◊Q. What can you do on a heart return at Trick 2? You can take the ♠A, ruff a spade and try a club towards the nine. However, the ten comes up, forcing the ace. You ruff another spade, but East hops up with the ♣K to play a third round of hearts to promote West's ◊Q. If instead you draw trumps and ruff a spade in dummy, East discards a club and then unblocks the ♠Q on the second spade to avoid being thrown in with it on the third. Again you finish a trick short.

HAND 15 SURPRISE RUN

After winning the first trick in hand, declarer could draw trumps with the king and queen and then run the diamond eight. East wins with the queen and safely exits with a spade. Now taking the ◇A and then ruffing a diamond sees West show out. Therefore, declarer goes over to dummy with an ace and takes the marked ruffing finesse in diamonds. One ace remains to provide access to the good diamond, which generates the twelfth trick. Can you see a way to do anything about this?

West needs to stay more alert. This defender has to recognize that declarer may intend to run the ◇8 and cover it, forcing out the ace. This brings us back to the failing lines we discussed earlier.

HAND 16 PLAIN SQUASH

After three rounds of diamonds, two rounds of spades and a diamond exit, West can beat you by leading the queen of hearts. Although this sets up the jack, you lack the entries to score three heart tricks and you will lose a club at the end. You will have to find a better plan if you want to make this contract.

If West had a doubleton in each major, you could secure a helpful return by cashing both your ace-kings before getting off play. In addition, without the spade blockage, you would be able to run four spade tricks and stand a much better chance of stripping the hand. Can you succeed on the actual layout?

You need to play East for the jack and ten of clubs. This does not seem so unlikely given what else you know about the hand. Moreover, you can forget about endplays and the like. A simple avoidance play will do the job. Unblock the ace-king of spades and lead the nine of clubs. East wins with the ten and returns a heart to your ace. You lead a low club, planning to duck if the missing low club appears (to cater for jack-ten doubleton on your right). In practice the king pops up, which simplifies matters. The ♣Q can now score your game-going trick.

HAND 17 WRONG GAME

To succeed in 4♠ you really require both the queen and jack of diamonds on your right. Take two rounds of trumps — with the jack then the ace — and lead a low diamond off dummy. East must play high to prevent you from winning with the nine, and you can capture the jack with the ace. Continue with the nine to the king to arrive at a decision point.

If East started with three diamonds, you want to lead low. To cater to the actual lie, you need to play the ten, pinning West's eight and picking up the queen via a ruffing finesse. The a priori odds make the four-card holding more probable, in broad terms by a factor of eight to six. The bidding provides another reason to try the ten. Giving West a 1-3-4-5 places five hearts with East, who had the chance to bid 2♡ yet failed to do so. A 1-4-4-4 shape seems equally unlikely: firstly, West might have pulled the redouble to 1NT; secondly, East would hardly overtake the club.

Yes, 3NT rolls in with nine top tricks, but staying out of your nine-card major-suit fit takes some doing.

HAND 18 DELIGHTFUL DILEMMA

If East puts up the ♣Q at Trick 1, declarer should duck. This makes it a simple matter to finesse the jack of clubs and draw precisely two rounds of trumps, the ideal number for removing West's but leaving one on the table. The fourth round of clubs ruffed with the ♡4 provides a tenth trick.

To defeat the contract, East should duck the opening lead, allowing the jack to win! This gives declarer a similar dilemma to the one that arose after taking the queen with the ace. Now one round of trumps followed by two rounds of clubs allows East to play a fourth club; West's uppercut with the ♡5 then promotes a trump trick. Taking both the queen of trumps as well as the ace before giving up a club lets East play a third round of trumps; after that, provided West ensures dummy's diamond entries do not remain intact (remember the danger of a double squeeze), declarer will have to lose a trick at the end.

HAND 19 LETHAL COCKTAIL

We have looked at the outcome if East plays a second heart or shifts to a spade, but neither move seems to work. What happens after a club at Trick 2? The strong desire to conserve the ♣A as an entry to the diamonds obliges declarer to play a high card from hand and, when the king appears, to duck in dummy.

West could persevere with clubs, but declarer can win the club in hand and drive out the ◇A. Clearly, a spade switch by West will bring no joy, since this would go round to the ace-queen. Instead, West should revert to hearts.

Declarer must hold up on the second round of hearts or go two down, losing four hearts and a trick in each minor. Now the spotlight returns to East. A club fails as the closed hand wins and a third round of hearts does not work either: with the long hearts and the ◇A in different hands, the contract makes. To succeed East has to switch once again, this time to spades. Two heart winners, and one in each of the other suits provide the five that the defenders require.

HAND 20 ACE APPEASEMENT

After the ◇K wins the opening lead and a low club appears at Trick 2, West should rise with the ♣A to continue diamonds. East takes the ace and plays a third diamond, forcing South to ruff high. It is now possible to go over to dummy with a club and play a trump, but what happens then? East can go up with the ♠A and persevere with a fourth round of diamonds. This proves a real killer.

To make 4♠ you need to cover the ◇9 with the queen. If East holds back the ace, dummy gains the lead and you can lead trumps towards your king-queen. If the ace captures the queen, you win the next diamond and, despite the strong 1NT opening, play a club to the king — the trump promotion would defeat you anyway if West had the ♣Q rather than the ace. Now you can safely lead a trump and, if East flies in with the ace to continue diamonds, afford to ruff high. In practice, West may well take the ♣A on the first round (lest you hold a singleton), removing any doubt about the club position.

MINIATURE 3. BROKEN HEARTS

Six hearts might be made if declarer can take four ruffs whilst the defenders follow suit and then has the lead in hand at Trick 11. At this point, the trump suit must look something like this:

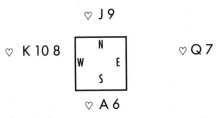

♡ J 9

♡ K 10 8   ♡ Q 7

♡ A 6

South's other remaining card must be in the same suit as East's but in a different suit to North's. Declarer leads this plain-suit card; West has to ruff high to stop dummy's jack from scoring but is then endplayed.

Clearly, the same circumstances bring success if West has K-10-7, Q-10-8 or Q-10-7. You could also succeed if West has K-Q-10, 10-8-7 or K-Q. A final scenario is that West has K-Q-8 or K-Q-7. In this case, West would again ruff high and exit low. By playing dummy's jack, you could make the contract, but this would have to be losing policy in the long run.

SECTION 5

Solutions for 'More Testing'

HAND 21 EXTRA VALUE

You can make 3NT by putting East in a dilemma. After taking the ♠A, and before touching the diamonds, lead a low club.

If West puts up the queen, you win in dummy, cash two diamonds and return the ♣10 (you could defer cashing the diamonds or lead a high heart off dummy before going back to clubs). If East takes the ♣J, your ♣9 becomes an entry to the diamonds. If not, you only require two heart tricks to go with two spades, three clubs and two diamonds, and can switch to hearts. West cannot prevent you from making that second spade trick. If need be, you exit with the fourth round of hearts (or clubs).

West probably ducks at Trick 2 and you insert dummy's ten. This brings us to much the same position as in the previous paragraph. If East wins the ten with the jack, your ♣9 serves as an entry to the diamonds once you have unblocked the ace and king. If not, the ♣10 scores and you can develop the two heart tricks you require at leisure.

HAND 22 JAILBREAK

Suppose you cash the ♣Q at Trick 2 and, on seeing West follow to the second round of clubs, overtake the jack with the king. You then play a diamond to the queen, which loses to the ace. You are fine if a spade comes back as you can win, finish the clubs, and later make the ◊J and your final spade winner. Alas, West catches you by surprise: a diamond goes to East's king and a club exit locks you in dummy. You can cash the rest of the clubs, but both defenders hang on to three hearts. You must attack hearts and are bound to lose three tricks in the suit.

To succeed you need to take the slight risk of four clubs on your right (you will have a marked finesse if they are on your left). Overtake the first round of clubs (low to the ace also works given the 3-2 split) and lead a diamond off dummy. This renders the defenders helpless. If they take their diamonds and return a club, you can win it in hand to enjoy your spade winners. You have a certain heart stopper and, if West continues spades, you pitch a heart from dummy and wait to score your third spade trick until after you have led a diamond towards the jack.

HAND 23 TERRIFIC TIMING

Once the ♣K loses to the ace and a trump comes back, you ruff a heart to hand. As entries to dummy look scarce, you could lead the ◇7 to the ace and ruff a second heart. You go back to the table with a trump and ruff a third heart. Although the ♡A falls, you have reached a hopeless position. You would have to exit with a club to escape for one down.

You need to set up a third diamond trick whilst you retain control over proceedings. After your initial heart ruff, lead the ◇7 and duck. You win the trump return in dummy, ruff another heart, draw the missing trump and cash the ◇K. Then lead the ◇10 to the ace, ruff a third heart and cross back by playing the carefully preserved ◇2 to the six. You can now enjoy the ♡K.

HAND 24 PROTECTING PARTNER

What happens if the play commences with three rounds of clubs and East discards a diamond? Declarer strips the diamonds and wins the first round of trumps in dummy. It appears tempting now to ruff another club and lead a low heart, playing for a 2-2 heart break. However, the 5-2 club split and West's takeout double make a 3-1 division much more probable. Therefore, declarer plays a fourth round of clubs but throws a spade, forcing West either to return a spade or concede a ruff and discard.

East might foresee the loser on loser play and ruff the fourth club. In this case, declarer overruffs, wins the second round of trumps in dummy (drawing the outstanding one in the process) and leads a spade, planning to cover the jack or otherwise insert the ten. West wins but is well and truly stuck.

We rewind to Trick 3 and this time East discards a spade. Still hoping for a 2-2 trump break, declarer takes the ace and king of hearts, ruffs the third diamond and tries a fourth round of clubs. If East throws a diamond, South sheds a spade and West is fixed. Ruffing also fails: it would allow declarer to overruff and lead the ♠K! Then the doubleton jack blocks the spades, which prevents the defenders from making three tricks in the suit. To beat the contract East must throw a second spade. Now West could escape by cashing the ♠A and giving East a spade ruff.

HAND 25 DISCARD DECISION

After a spade to the ace, a heart to the ace and three further rounds of spades, declarer should throw a diamond. East may persevere with a fifth round of spades, in which case the power of the ♣10 comes into play. West can ruff but dummy overruffs and there is no trump promotion.

To beat the contract West must throw the ◇8 and ◇J on the second and third rounds of spades. East carries on with a fourth round of spades and it does declarer no good to pitch a diamond now. West can also get rid of a diamond — the ace! On a diamond switch now, South ruffs low, but West can overruff for a one-trick set and applause from the kibitzers.

Note that if declarer draws trumps at Tricks 2 to 4 before trying a diamond, West grabs the ace and leads the ♡J. East ducks and always has an exit card in spades. Again it is one down.

If you thought that was spectacular, see what you make of this:

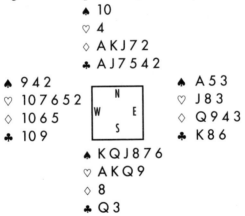

```
              ♠ 10
              ♡ 4
              ◇ A K J 7 2
              ♣ A J 7 5 4 2
 ♠ 9 4 2                    ♠ A 5 3
 ♡ 10 7 6 5 2      N        ♡ J 8 3
 ◇ 10 6 5       W     E     ◇ Q 9 4 3
 ♣ 10 9            S        ♣ K 8 6
              ♠ K Q J 8 7 6
              ♡ A K Q 9
              ◇ 8
              ♣ Q 3
```

South plays in 6♠ and West leads the ♣10. Declarer goes up with dummy's ace and throws the club queen on the second diamond. Then come four rounds of hearts, the last ruffed with the ♠10. Overruffing fails and East fares no better by discarding from one of the minors. Declarer can enter hand by ruffing that minor and again the defenders have no way to promote West's ♠9. To beat the slam East must underruff, take the first spade and then lead the minor suit that South ruffed at Trick 8.

HAND 26 SENSITIVE STRIP

To make 4♠ you need to restrict your losses to two hearts and a club; you avoid the diamond loser by forcing East to give you a ruff and discard. Moreover, you must take care that West never gets in lead to cash a diamond and that East does not win a second heart until you are ready.

You can afford to draw three rounds of trumps and then play ace of clubs followed by a club to the jack. Your finger-crossing or whatever you do in these situations works. East wins the trick and probably returns a club. You ruff and then advance the ♡9, intending to run it. If West covers, dummy's ace wins and you give up two heart tricks. If not, you lose the first heart trick, win the second, and lose the third. Either way you achieve your goal. East has only rounded-suit cards left, allowing you to ruff the next trick in dummy whilst shedding a diamond from hand.

A similar position results if East leads a heart after taking the second round of clubs. You put in the nine and play dummy's ace if and only if West contributes the queen. Whether it takes the first or second round of the suit, the ♡A serves as an entry for you to ruff a club in hand. You can then exit with a heart as above. Note that playing two rounds of clubs before pulling trumps also works. It takes an initial heart lead to beat you.

Here is another example of spot cards in a vital role in an endplay:

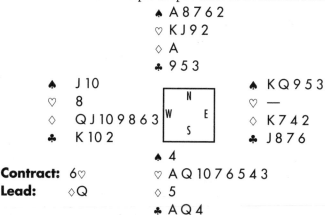

```
                  ♠ A 8 7 6 2
                  ♡ K J 9 2
                  ◇ A
                  ♣ 9 5 3
      ♠  J 10              ♠  K Q 9 5 3
      ♡  8          N      ♡  —
      ◇  Q J 10 9 8 6 3  W   E  ◇  K 7 4 2
      ♣  K 10 2      S      ♣  J 8 7 6
                  ♠ 4
Contract: 6♡        ♡ A Q 10 7 6 5 4 3
Lead:    ◇Q         ◇ 5
                  ♣ A Q 4
```

Declarer takes the ◇A, the ♡A and the ♠A and calls for the ♠2. If East plays high, there is a double ruffing finesse; if not, South throws the ♣4 to fix West.

HAND 27 RED HERRING

Knowing that a heart return offers complete safety, you should deduce from East's ♣J shift that the king lies over your queen. In this case, if you give up on trying to score a trick with the ◇10 (because you need the ◇J onside and a helpful trump layout), the only hope left is a squeeze. The diamond threat sits in dummy, which means that you should select West as your victim. This makes covering the ♣J unwise. Indeed, it would only prove right if West has ♣K-4 doubleton and East the long diamonds, in which case your ♣5 would become the club threat. However, then the ♣J shift would be a mistake — it gives you the chance to transfer the club guard from West to East, a play for which you would lack the entry on a passive heart return.

After letting the club run round to dummy's ace, you call for the major-suit aces next and then use the final ace, diamonds, as an entry for ruffing a heart. You must ruff high in dummy, not for fear of an overruff, but because you want to run the trumps and cannot afford to block them at this stage.

You are pleased to find three trumps on your right since this clearly increases the chance of long diamonds on your left. As you lead the last trump, this is the position:

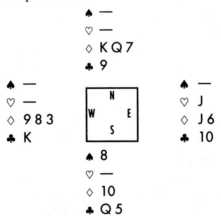

West has no answer.

HAND 28 OMAR'S DISCARD

Omar observed West's play of the two of clubs. He knew his partner had a choice of clubs to play and interpreted this tiny spot card as a suit-preference signal, denying heart values. Therefore, he decided to focus on winning two trump tricks and pitched a diamond at Trick 3. His opponent gratefully won with the queen, crossed to dummy with a diamond and took the spade finesse. However, Omar ruffed the next diamond and exited with a heart, leaving declarer unable to pick up the ♠K.

At the table, throwing a diamond on the third club guaranteed the contract's defeat, but I have changed the hand slightly to give declarer a counter. Before playing a second diamond, cash the ace-king of hearts. East can ruff the second diamond and return a heart. Yes, you must ruff this in hand, but you can overruff in dummy! This allows you to repeat the spade finesse and make ten tricks.

HAND 29 ENLIST THE ENEMY

You cannot make 4♠ by running the trumps. You have to use the ♣K as a re-entry to get back to hand and East can simply keep two diamonds and three clubs. Whether you keep three clubs and two diamonds in dummy or the other way round you will lose two tricks in each minor.

Before admitting defeat, you should consider another way to arrive at ten tricks. If you can get a long club and the ◇Q, you only need five trump tricks. Have you spotted the answer now?

Draw one round of trumps by leading the five to the ace, then play three rounds of clubs, ruffing high. Next, still saving the ♠2, cross back to dummy with a trump, and ruff another club high. If West has shown out on the second trump, you could be sure of the position. You would play your last big trump and exit with the ♠2, knowing East will win. On the actual layout you need to hope that the missing trump lies on your right and lead the ♠2 at Trick 8, risking two down if it turns up on your left.

Note that you also make the contract on the above line with clubs 3-3. In this case, East will have to ruff the fourth club. If another trump is still out, you overruff and exit with the ♠2. Otherwise you discard (or even underruff) to leave the defender on play.

HAND 30 MAJOR DEVELOPMENT

Assuming standard leads, declarer will surely let the spade run round to the closed hand. In practice East takes the king in third seat and must decide what to do. A spade return will be too slow: East cannot continue spades and West holds only one possible entry, the ♣A. Might a heart switch do the trick?

Clearly a low heart lead brings little joy — at least not to the player who makes it. An alert declarer hops up with the ten and probably plays on clubs. West may win the first club and try a second heart, but dummy's ace (or a low card) deals with that.

What happens if East prefers the heart king at Trick 2? This renders the ♡10 useless. However, declarer can allow the ♡K to hold and the defenders make just two kings and two clubs.

To defeat 3NT East must shift to the ♡J. If the queen takes this, West wins the first club and continues the heart attack, setting up two heart tricks. If the ♡J holds, East exits passively and again West grabs the first round of clubs to play a heart. Either way two hearts, a spade and two clubs are enough.

Could it ever be right to switch to your top card? Take a look at this:

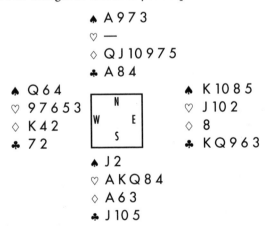

```
                    ♠ A 9 7 3
                    ♡ —
                    ◊ Q J 10 9 7 5
                    ♣ A 8 4
    ♠ Q 6 4                          ♠ K 10 8 5
    ♡ 9 7 6 5 3      N               ♡ J 10 2
    ◊ K 4 2        W   E             ◊ 8
    ♣ 7 2            S               ♣ K Q 9 6 3
                    ♠ J 2
                    ♡ A K Q 8 4
                    ◊ A 6 3
                    ♣ J 10 5
```

South plays in 3NT having shown 15-17 and five hearts. East wins the club lead with the queen and must switch to the ♠K. If the ace is played first or second time, the defenders make three spades, a club and a diamond; if not, West reverts to clubs and holds up the ◊ K to kill dummy. The ♠10 fails as all cover and dummy's 9-7-3 will provide a stopper.

HAND 31 PASSIVE POTENTIAL

With tenace holdings in both minors, common sense suggests a winning throw in lies out there somewhere. Of the options that we did not discuss earlier, playing ace and another club clearly fails. East will get in with the ♣Q and make the deadly diamond shift.

To succeed you need to attack diamonds, and to use the spot cards to their full potential. If East plays low on the first round of diamonds, you insert the nine, thrusting the lead on to West. On the likely low club shift, you go up with the jack from dummy and later lead towards the ten. You can cater for a diamond exit or a ruff and discard equally well.

East does better to play high on the first round of diamonds. It seems tempting to cover with the king, but West can capture it with the ace and escape by returning a low diamond. Instead you should duck and cover the next diamond. Now when West takes the ace and tries a low diamond, you pitch a club from dummy, letting the lead come round to your nine. Of course, neither defender could gain by playing a heart or club instead.

The diamond combination above has a first cousin as we now see:

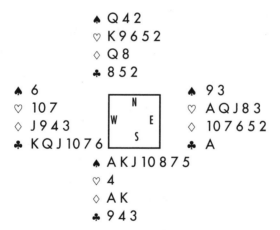

```
              ♠ Q 4 2
              ♡ K 9 6 5 2
              ◊ Q 8
              ♣ 8 5 2
    ♠ 6                     ♠ 9 3
    ♡ 10 7          N       ♡ A Q J 8 3
    ◊ J 9 4 3    W     E    ◊ 10 7 6 5 2
    ♣ K Q J 10 7 6    S     ♣ A
              ♠ A K J 10 8 7 5
              ♡ 4
              ◊ A K
              ♣ 9 4 3
```

West, who opened 3♣, leads the ♣K against 4♠. East overtakes with the ace and switches to the ◊5. West's high clubs and dummy's lack of entries dictate the best line. Declarer cashes two ace-kings and tries to play a heart to dummy's nine. West does best to rise with the ten, but the king covers this and East is stuck after being allowed two heart tricks.

HAND 32 CANNED HEAT

You can make 3NT — by means of a progressive squeeze. You have threats against West in three suits and, once the defender unguards one of these, you should gain a new squeeze card. However, to bring it all together you must take great care.

You want to reduce the loser count as much as possible. Therefore, you hold up the ♠A until the fourth round. At this point, provided you have kept all the hearts and at least five diamonds in dummy, West already finds the pressure too much:

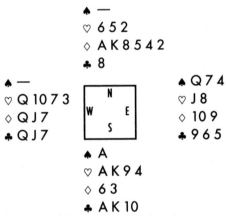

```
                ♠ —
                ♡ 6 5 2
                ◇ A K 8 5 4 2
                ♣ 8
    ♠ —                       ♠ Q 7 4
    ♡ Q 10 7 3     N          ♡ J 8
    ◇ Q J 7     W     E       ◇ 10 9
    ♣ Q J 7        S          ♣ 9 6 5
                ♠ A
                ♡ A K 9 4
                ◇ 6 3
                ♣ A K 10
```

West can ill afford to discard a diamond — doing this would concede several tricks. We next consider the impact of a heart discard.

Dummy can spare any low red card, and you can simply play ace, king and a third heart. North's ◇A deals with a switch to the ◇Q and you come back to hand with a club. The long heart then squeezes West in the minors.

A club discard from West proves more testing. Indeed, since East could easily hold the ten of clubs rather than the nine, you should expect a good defender to try this. Three rounds of clubs squeeze West down to three hearts and now you understand the need to preserve dummy's hearts. You go over to the ◇A and play a heart, sticking in the nine if East follows low or covering the jack. Either way you safely duck a heart into the hand on your left. In the latter case, West may drop the ten, and you can then continue with the ♡9 (or succeed with an endplay).

HAND 33 DOUBLETON KING

By itself, holding up the ♣A will not prevent the trump promotion. East is the one with the trump king and long clubs. Indeed, the way the cards lie, the defenders will come to a second trump trick in one form or another. However, it gets declarer off to a start.

After winning the second club, you can cash the ♠A but must then hope for a 3-3 diamond break. You play four rounds of the suit, throwing a club. West can ruff but has no way to get East in to obtain a second ruff. Equally East may elect to trump the diamond and play a club, enabling West to overruff, but again you can get in to pull the last trump

HAND 34 DIVIDE AND RULE

Once you have drawn trumps and played a diamond to the queen, you could lead the ◇J from hand next. The bidding makes it rather unlikely that East started with a doubleton ace of diamonds. Alas, the extra trump retained in dummy brings no real benefit. East can win the diamond and play a club through. Holding three clubs, the hand on your left can always escape an endplay and you go down whether or not you finesse.

To succeed you must lead a low diamond off dummy at Trick 2. This carries little risk. West might have preferred a singleton diamond lead to a trump. In any case, if East hops up with the ◇A and gives West a ruff, you are well placed with the trumps 2-1. A lead into your rounded-suit tenaces will cover one potential loser and the ◇K the other.

East ducks the diamond and your queen wins. You draw the missing trump and play a diamond to your jack. At this point you resist playing a third diamond. Instead, you must play a trump, followed by a heart to the nine (or you cover the queen). West scores two heart tricks but then has to surrender. It would not matter if West could exit with a diamond to East's ace: then the long diamond would take care of your club loser. If the worst comes to the worst and East turns up with something like Q-10-x of hearts, you can still fall back on the club finesse. This line only backfires if East can win the second heart, the club finesse fails, and diamonds were 3-3 all along.

HAND 35 HIDDEN ENTRY

After a heart to the ten and king, and a club to the ace, suppose West plays ace and another heart. East cannot spare a club, though a spade looks safe. With the hearts ready to run, West is now the danger hand and declarer needs to tread carefully. Cashing two top clubs after winning the spade switch proves fatal as this sets up two club winners for East.

To succeed from here declarer leaves a high club in dummy and leads a diamond towards hand. If East goes in up with the king, the natural avoidance play of ducking lands the contract without further ado. If the defender prefers to play low, declarer can finesse the queen, cross back to dummy with a spade and repeat the process. As well as three diamonds, two spades, two hearts and a club, another trick will come in the wash.

To beat 3NT East has to throw the ◇K on the third heart. It looks like declarer can collect nine tricks by knocking out the ♠Q, but the act of cashing dummy's clubs lets the defenders score five first: three clubs, the ♠Q and the ♡A. Leaving a club winner on the table works no better.

A more flamboyant illustration of the same theme arises on this deal:

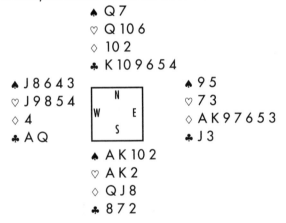

```
              ♠ Q 7
              ♡ Q 10 6
              ◇ 10 2
              ♣ K 10 9 6 5 4
♠ J 8 6 4 3                      ♠ 9 5
♡ J 9 8 5 4        N             ♡ 7 3
◇ 4            W       E         ◇ A K 9 7 6 5 3
♣ A Q             S             ♣ J 3
              ♠ A K 10 2
              ♡ A K 2
              ◇ Q J 8
              ♣ 8 7 2
```

Contract 3NT
Lead   ◇4

East opens 3◇ and South's 3NT overcall buys the contract. East wins Trick 1 with the ◇K and continues with the ace and three. Both the bidding and East's lowly ◇3 mark South with both major-suit ace-kings. West must take the only chance and discard the queen and ace of clubs.

HAND 36 FATAL CHOICE

To have any real hope of ruffing a diamond in dummy you must draw two rounds of trumps using South's top cards. With the ace gone, West could ruff in with the ♠10 on the second diamond. This creates another problem.

Suppose you take the ◇A, the king-queen of spades, four top hearts and ruff a diamond with the ♠A. You now want to return to the South hand to extract West's remaining trump, but you are in danger of running into a trump promotion. Sure, if East holds a singleton club or West the K-Q-J, you survive playing ace and another club. Normally, and as the cards lie, East can get in and play a deadly third round of diamonds.

Although you cannot always guarantee to keep East out, you can prevail on the present layout. Whilst you still have a re-entry in one of the majors, lead a club to the ace. If East retains the ♣K, you run the hearts and concede a club before taking the diamond ruff. If East unblocks the ♣K, only West can win a club exit and you can safely ruff a diamond first.

Careful timing also circumvents a trump promotion on this example:

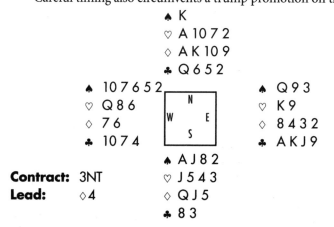

```
                  ♠ K
                  ♡ A 10 7 2
                  ◇ A K 10 9
                  ♣ Q 6 5 2
  ♠ 10 7 6 5 2                      ♠ Q 9 3
  ♡ Q 8 6              N            ♡ K 9
  ◇ 7 6          W          E       ◇ 8 4 3 2
  ♣ 10 7 4              S           ♣ A K J 9
                  ♠ A J 8 2
Contract:  3NT    ♡ J 5 4 3
Lead:      ◇4     ◇ Q J 5
                  ♣ 8 3
```

East, who opened 1♣, wins Trick 1 with the ♣J and continues with the ace and king. Declarer ruffs and, knowing West would lead the ten from ♣10-9-7-4, has to hope West has three hearts. The winning line is to unblock the ♠A, come over with a diamond, throw dummy's club on the ♠A and advance the ♡J. Best is for East to win and play the fourth club anyway, but declarer ruffs in hand and West cannot take a trick.

HAND 37 EITHER WAY

Having decided that each defender has a top spade, you can never score a spade ruff by cashing two big trumps before losing two rounds of spades. The reason is that the ♡A provides the only entry to dummy's clubs, which means you must play one round of trumps yourself. For a start, you have to hope that whoever holds the doubleton trump will follow to four rounds of clubs. Moreover, as you are bound to get a trump switch to knock out the ♡K after you concede the first spade, you should aim to stop the defender with the third trump winning the second spade.

Put up dummy's ◇A, unblock the clubs, cross to the ♡A, say your prayers, and play two more rounds of clubs. West discards a diamond on the fourth club, which tells you the longer trump holding is also there. In this case, you broach spades with a low card off dummy. If East puts up the king to protect West's entry, you no longer need a spade ruff. If it was East who showed out on the fourth club, you would play spades the other way, ruffing a diamond to enter the South hand and then leading up to the queen. Either way you score a spade trick or a spade ruff.

HAND 38 SEVENTH HEAVEN

If the play starts with a club to the jack and queen, the ♠10 to the king and a spade back, overtaking with the ace works. Declarer pulls trumps and attacks diamonds. West gets in only once and, assuming dummy covers the second club lead, cannot both play a club through the king and dislodge the ♠Q. Have you seen another (and superior) route to eight tricks? Unblock the ♠9 at Trick 2 and then it matters not if West turns up with both big diamonds. Does this mean 2♡ should always make?

The bidding marks South with four spades because without them a transfer (or weak take-out) would be more appropriate. Therefore, East has no need to return a high spade to signal a doubleton. A switch to the ♠7 allows the defenders to take the ♠K, lead a club through the king and play a second spade. If declarer wins this in dummy and ruffs a club, the defenders will later take the first diamond, cash a second and exit with a club. If the ♠A captures the second spade, West will win the first round of diamonds and play a third spade to remove dummy's entry.

HAND 39 POWERFUL POSITION

After a heart goes to the nine and jack, East shifts to a trump, allowing West to play queen, ace and another. Declarer could now discard two clubs on the diamonds and ruff one in dummy, but this still leaves one club loser. Trying to set up a heart trick seems a forlorn hope. East will cover the king or follow small on a low card.

With the three tricks already lost, only a squeeze can save the day. The heart position offers great potential as both defenders must protect the suit. Still, you need to get the timing right to bring off a double ruffing squeeze.

If you win the third spade and run four diamonds straight away, nobody feels much pressure. Somebody keeps three clubs and you go down. You should take Trick 4 in dummy and ruff the ♡3. Now this position results as you play the fourth round of diamonds:

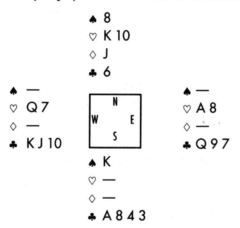

```
              ♠ 8
              ♡ K 10
              ◇ J
              ♣ 6
  ♠ —                        ♠ —
  ♡ Q 7         N            ♡ A 8
  ◇ —        W     E         ◇ —
  ♣ K J 10       S           ♣ Q 9 7
              ♠ K
              ♡ —
              ◇ —
              ♣ A 8 4 3
```

East could pitch a heart, which would allow you to ruff out the ace, but is more likely to release a club. A club goes from the South hand and West feels the pinch. Throwing a heart would permit you to play the ♡K next for a ruffing finesse, while coming down to two clubs enables you to ruff out the clubs. Indeed, whatever the defenders do at this point, the contract makes.

HAND 40 ENCHANTING ENDPLAYS

After ruffing the third round of diamonds, drawing trumps and cashing two hearts, you should play a low club from each hand. If the suit breaks 3-2, you can take the marked finesse on the next round. If East wins with a singleton and concedes a ruff and discard, you trump in hand and can then finesse the clubs. If West goes in with the nine of clubs, a return of the ten no longer provides a means of escape. The queen and seven have suddenly become equals and you can pick up the king.

Can you still the make the contract if East switches to a club after the second diamond? You play high from hand and West has to cover or you will just duck a club later. After the ace wins, you draw trumps, cash a second club (not essential as the cards lie) and take the ace and king of hearts. You now play dummy's ◇10, pitching a club. East has only red cards left and must lead one of them, allowing you to throw a second club from hand and ruff in dummy. It is equally simple if the club switch comes at Trick 2. Then you can win the second heart in either hand and give up two diamond tricks, your ◇J keeping West off play.

HAND 41 SAVAGE SWITCH

West wants to reduce the threat of spade ruffs without losing control over the subsequent play. It is possible to achieve this by switching to the ◇6, a move Marc Smith spotted. Declarer can ruff one spade on the table, but then West will be able to cash a spade after getting in with the ◇A. Setting up the clubs seems little better. If you draw trumps after ruffing the third club, the defenders will score two spade tricks. If you leave two trumps out, somebody will definitely be in a position to ruff a good club with a low trump. Can you envisage the solution?

You can win the trump switch in either hand and play three rounds of clubs, ruffing high. If West overruffs and tries a spade, you ruff in dummy and play a winning club, collecting East's last trump. Assuming West discards, you cross to the ♡A and play a master club anyway. You overruff (if East ruffs) or else discard a spade. Whatever the defenders do, you get to throw one spade on a club and ruff the other in dummy. Yes, you need friendly breaks, but remember nobody doubled you in 5◇.

HAND 42 SELFLESS DEVOTION

East should duck the heart lead off dummy, and as smoothly as possible — declarer might have the king-jack of hearts and a view to take. As it happens, there is no guess and, provided South did not carelessly use the ♠K-Q to draw trumps, it proves a simple matter to ruff both hearts on the table. Clearly, making a loser on loser play on the third heart serves little purpose. The ♡A must reside with East, who can lead diamonds safely. Declarer does best to take three rounds of clubs and then play a diamond off dummy. The ♢9 is the correct card in the hope that West holds the jack-ten. However, East can cover the nine with the jack or put the eight on a low card. This thwarts the throw in and places the contract at the mercy of the diamond finesse. It all goes to show how much bridge is a partnership game: East takes one trick and the slam makes, none and it goes one down.

HAND 43 HEARTLESS RETORT

Knowing the lead is a singleton, East should return the ♣10 at Trick 2. If West misreads this as a signal for hearts and tries the ♡K after ruffing the ♣Q, it will be allowed win. Again this corrects the loser count for the double squeeze. Declarer just has to remember to cash the ♡A while there is still a route back to hand in trumps, and we get to an identical end position to the one we saw earlier. Instead West should switch to a small diamond after ruffing the club, which dummy's ace takes. On the simple run of the trumps from here, nobody comes under pressure. If declarer ducks a heart at some point, West can play a second diamond, killing dummy's last entry and, with it, any squeeze chances. Alas, even all this fails to defeat the contract. Can you spot the reason why?

Dummy's ace takes the diamond shift and declarer can afford to draw one round of trumps with the ace. After that comes a diamond to the king and a diamond ruffed high, the ♡Q to the king and ace followed by a heart ruffed high. Finally, a trump to the nine (hence the high ruffing earlier) puts the lead in dummy for the master stroke: the ♡9 from dummy for a club pitch. West has to win and must concede a ruff and discard. Declarer's final club goes away whilst dummy ruffs.

HAND 44 BAD BREAK

You cannot make the contract if you ruff the diamond and cash a top trump. If you continue with king and another heart, East forces you with a diamond and you will go two down. As we saw previously, turning to clubs after one round of trumps also results in failure. East can always stop the clubs by ruffing and then can exit with a trump or, when they have gone, with a diamond.

To make game you must foresee the danger of a 4-0 trump split and lead a low heart at Trick 2. Just about the only time this could backfire comes if both defenders hold a black-suit void — very unlikely. As the cards lie, East perforce wins the first trump and plays a second round of diamonds, which forces you to ruff. You might guess what to do next. Yes, you duck a second trump as well. Dummy's third trump protects you against further diamond leads and you will be able to run the clubs in peace.

Would you like to see an example of ducking with one fewer trump?

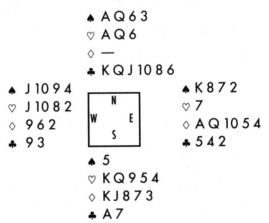

```
               ♠ A Q 6 3
               ♡ A Q 6
               ◇ —
               ♣ K Q J 10 8 6
  ♠ J 10 9 4                    ♠ K 8 7 2
  ♡ J 10 8 2        N           ♡ 7
  ◇ 9 6 2      W        E       ◇ A Q 10 5 4
  ♣ 9 3             S           ♣ 5 4 2
               ♠ 5
               ♡ K Q 9 5 4
               ◇ K J 8 7 3
               ♣ A 7
```

Contract: 6♡

Opening Lead: ♠J

To cater for a 4-1 trump break and a doubleton club in the hand with four trumps, you should duck a heart at Trick 2. Barring awful breaks, you can use the ♣A and a spade ruff as entries to ruff one diamond in dummy and get back to hand to finish drawing trumps. As the cards lie, if you do anything else, you go down. Try it and see.

HAND 45 HELPFUL SPLIT?

If declarer ruffs the club, cashes the ◇A, crosses to the ♡A and returns a diamond, East can ruff the second or third round and play a trump to cut out any ruffs in dummy. The contract must fail from here: even if West had no spades above the eight, East still has an exit card in clubs, which prevents an effective endplay.

To succeed you forget all about diamond ruffs and strip the hand instead. Ruff the first club, cross to the ♡A, ruff another club, go back to the ♡Q and ruff a third club. With any luck, this sequence will exhaust East's supply of clubs. Can you spot the key move after you have drawn the missing trump and cashed the ◇A?

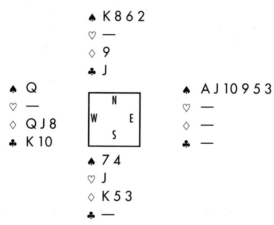

Rarely do you open up the suit with which you intend to throw in an opponent, yet you need to do precisely that here. Duck a spade! If East wins cheaply (not that this can happen as the cards lie), you should get a kind spade return to set up dummy's king. In practice, West wins and can do no better than to try a diamond. Thanks to your having kept one top diamond, you can win this and play a spade to the eight (or you might play the last trump to give East the chance to pitch a club). You throw a diamond on the ♠A return and the ♠K scores the game-going trick.

HAND 46 TIMELY LOSS

We recap the proposed play to date: a heart to the king, a trump back, a diamond to West, a second trump, another diamond to West and a third trump, followed by three more trumps. Even though only one defender can guard the minors, defending the end position proves comfortable. After declarer's trumps are gone, everyone will still hold four cards. Therefore, West can keep three clubs and the ◊A. East merely needs to retain the ♡A.

From declarer's point of view, there is clearly no mileage in trying to ruff out the clubs. The ♠6 will only provide a late entry if the trumps split 2-2, in which case ruffing a diamond also works. No, only a squeeze can save the day. You just need to get the timing right.

Once East shows out on the second round of trumps (i.e. at Trick 4), you have to abandon the idea of ruffing diamonds. You can foresee that West will remove dummy's last trump if you play a second diamond and must instead take the opportunity to lose a heart. East wins and probably plays a diamond (you could cope with a club either by guessing the club position or by taking it in dummy and playing a diamond yourself). You hold back the king, which allows West to win cheaply and play a third round of trumps. Now when you run the trumps, this position results:

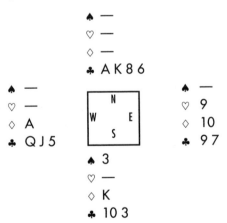

This time, West has no safe discard on the last spade.

HAND 47 ELUSIVE EXIT

You will recall that after the ♠Q held, three rounds of trumps followed and then three rounds of clubs, leaving the lead in dummy to play a diamond. If East follows low, South should stick in the eight, saving the queen for use later. A diamond return now looks fatal, but might West escape by conceding a ruff and discard? Indeed, whether North or South ruffs the contract fails. Spotting this, declarer discards a spade from both hands! Now the poor defender has to play a diamond into the A-Q.

East ought to rise with the ten on the first diamond lead. Once more, the play of the queen results in failure. West could win with the king and exit with either a club or a high diamond. To get home, declarer needs to capture the ◊10 with the ace and then try the ◊8, pitching a spade from dummy. Luckily, East was dealt only one diamond above the eight and cannot take the trick. West wins and can only delay the evil moment by playing the thirteenth club. Declarer counters by throwing a spade from both hands and waiting for a diamond lead to set up the queen.

HAND 48 RIGHTFUL RUFFING

After winning the second club and ruffing the diamonds good, declarer can advance the queen of spades. The king has to cover this, and then comes a fourth round of diamonds. It might look right for the defender with fewer trumps to ruff, just as was the case if a low trump went to the ace, but not here. If East ruffs, one of the defensive trump winners disappears.

Of course, West will have to ruff the diamond if East elects not to, leaving them with only one trump apiece. These would tumble together if declarer could play a second round of trumps; luckily for the them, West has the lead. To take advantage, East must dispose of a club on the diamond. Now if South throws a heart, West cashes the ♡A and the ♣J before playing a fourth round of clubs for East to ruff. A club discard on the diamond tests the defenders a little more. West needs to underlead the ♡A and win the heart return with the king before continuing clubs. Either way declarer helplessly underruffs and goes one down.

HAND 49 GUESS AVOIDED

The flat North hand and the singleton in the South hand suggest a dummy reversal. The snag is that the bidding warns of a 3-5 heart split, which makes ruffing the fourth round of hearts rather awkward. If you play East for three trumps, a diamond switch at Trick 2 will leave you an entry short for getting back to draw the last trump. You would need West to have bid 1NT on a 2-3-2-6 shape, in which case you could afford to leave the last trump out.

In fact trumping three hearts does provide the solution, or at least part of it. With any luck, it is West who holds three trumps and you can arrange for the loss of a trump trick to result in an endplay.

You should win the diamond switch in dummy, ruff a heart, cross over with the ♠Q and ruff another heart. Next cash the ♠K, play the ◇Q and a diamond to the ace. If West could ruff, you do not mind: you must get a club return. As the cards lie, all follow and ruffing the fourth heart presents the defender with a sad choice:

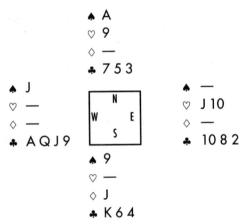

West can overruff and lead a club, allowing both the ♣K and the ◇J to score. If West discards, the ♠9 is a trick and you continue with the ◇J throwing a club from dummy; then either the ◇J or the ♣K will score.

You could also make the contract by using the ♠K to ruff the fourth round of hearts, winning the third diamond in dummy and exiting with a trump. The trap to avoid is using the diamond entry first. This would then force you to guess whether West is 3-3-3-4 or 3-3-2-5; play the wrong number of diamonds and you go down.

HAND 50 EASTERN ESCAPE

If East leads a club after winning the second round of trumps, the ♣K will take a trick. After that, ruffing two clubs in dummy deals with South's remaining losers — 5♠ doubled made.

Exiting with a heart works far better and the normal tactic of ruffing in the short trump hand will fail; with the ♣A offside, there are still two club losers. Therefore, declarer may ruff the heart in hand and throw a club from dummy. Now a club to the king and ace puts East back in the hot seat. A club exit at this point will allow the ♣J to score and two club ruffs will see the contract home. To succeed East needs to persevere with a fourth round of hearts. The North-South trumps make separately, but one of the defenders scores the last trick.

On that deal, East twice gave declarer a ruff and discard. We can go one better:

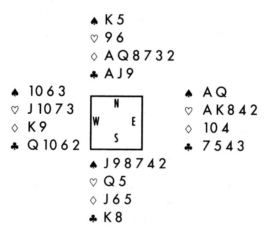

```
              ♠ K 5
              ♡ 9 6
              ◇ A Q 8 7 3 2
              ♣ A J 9
  ♠ 10 6 3              ♠ A Q
  ♡ J 10 7 3     N      ♡ A K 8 4 2
  ◇ K 9      W     E    ◇ 10 4
  ♣ Q 10 6 2     S      ♣ 7 5 4 3
              ♠ J 9 8 7 4 2
              ♡ Q 5
              ◇ J 6 5
              ♣ K 8
```

After East overcalls in hearts and East-West compete to 3♡, South arrives in 3♠. With the defenders unable to score either tricks or ruffs in the minors, their only winning strategy is to lead hearts and play a heart every time they get the chance. This promotes the ♠10. They should be able to find this because West, having led the ♡J, will drop the neutral ♡7 on the second round. This should help East to work out that a third trump trick offers the best hope of defeating the contract.

With little else to try, you put up the ♡A and rattle off the trumps. You must keep three diamonds in dummy as well as three clubs; all the hearts can go. East can spare one card in each minor and, as the final trump hits the deck, you picture this ending:

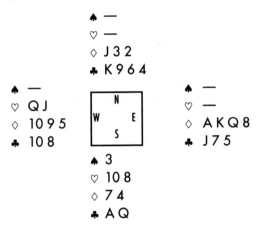

West does best to continue saving three diamonds, and parts with either a club or the ♡J. As planned, you discard a club from dummy and now the squeeze really bites.

If East throws a small diamond, you cash the ace and queen of clubs before exiting with a diamond. The poor defender can reel off three diamond winners but then must surrender the last trick to dummy's ♣K.

To avoid being used as a stepping-stone, East may prefer to get rid of a big diamond on the last trump. Two rounds of clubs no longer works because West can gain the lead in diamonds. To succeed you cash the ace of clubs only (indeed you could have played the ♣A earlier) and proceed to overtake the ♣Q with the king. Then you concede the third round of clubs to East. You lose two diamonds, but dummy's ◇J scores the last trick.

Note that this line works whenever East holds ◇A-K-Q and either at least four clubs or ♣J-10-x. You should always be able to read the end position.

HAND 52 BRILLIANT BATTLE

To make 4♠ you must go back to Trick 3. After taking the heart switch with dummy's ace, ruff a heart to hand (or you may cash one top club first). Then go across to the clubs and ruff the third round, on which East sheds a heart. Are you getting warm now?

With five trumps missing, you cannot possibly draw trumps ending in dummy to run the clubs. Nor can you score a long diamond (since the opening lead marks East with A-K-J-10) or, as we established earlier, ruff a diamond in dummy. Even so, you should play a diamond to sever the link between the opposing hands. East must return a trump and you win this in dummy to play a club. What can the defenders do?

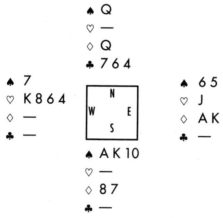

```
              ♠ Q
              ♡ —
              ◇ Q
              ♣ 7 6 4
  ♠ 7                        ♠ 6 5
  ♡ K 8 6 4      N           ♡ J
  ◇ —          W   E         ◇ A K
  ♣ —            S           ♣ —
              ♠ A K 10
              ♡ —
              ◇ 8 7
              ♣ —
```

If East ruffs, you overruff high and play a trump to dummy; this draws the missing trumps and you can run the clubs. If East discards, you pitch a diamond; then West ruffs and the enforced heart return allows you to crossruff the rest of the tricks.

Note that you could also get home from this position if you placed West with three trumps (e.g. if East had overcalled 1♡ and again turned up with 4-2 in the minors). In this case, having overruffed high you would concede a diamond. West could only prevent the diamond ruff by ruffing in, but then you would win the second trump in dummy and cash a club.

One discarding strategy for declarer is to throw a spade, a diamond and the ♣A from hand and two diamonds and a spade from dummy. This would be the position before the fourth round of clubs:

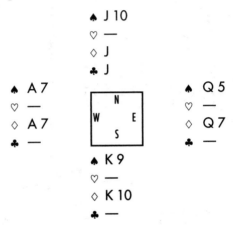

```
                        ♠ J 10
                        ♡ —
                        ◇ J
                        ♣ J
        ♠ A 7                             ♠ Q 5
        ♡ —          ┌─────────┐          ♡ —
        ◇ A 7        │ W   N   E │        ◇ Q 7
        ♣ —          │       S   │        ♣ —
                     └─────────┘
                        ♠ K 9
                        ♡ —
                        ◇ K 10
                        ♣ —
```

On the ♣J, East must throw a diamond (the suit in which dummy is short) and we have a suicide squeeze. Whichever suit South discards, West discards the opposite and the defenders take the last three tricks.

Could declarer do better by abandoning the long club and running the ♠J instead? In this case, East ducks, letting West win with the ace and exit with a spade. Declarer must then play diamonds from hand. It is clearly no better to lead the ◇J at Trick 10; East can even afford to cover.

You will notice that in this diagram both defenders have kept a pair of doubletons and this represents their optimum strategy. If either reduced to a singleton, declarer could play on that suit and make an extra trick.

Finally, suppose declarer keeps a 3-3 fit for the ending (spades for preference) and gives up on clubs a round earlier. In this case, it is vital that East has kept three spades and two diamonds. Then, after this defender ducks the ♠J and South unblocks the ♠9, West must win with the ace and exit in diamonds. There is then no way to reach dummy either to cash any further club winners or to repeat the spade finesse. All roads lead to a penalty of 800 (or 500 non-vulnerable).

SECTION 6

Solutions for 'Tougher Still'

HAND 53 SURPRISE SOLUTION

You can succeed in 6♠ but to do so you have to make West's seemingly certain trump trick disappear. You need to strip the hand and arrange for East to lead a suit (hearts no doubt) in which you have a void in both hands. This will give you the option to overruff West's ♠J in dummy.

To achieve the desired ending, you ruff a heart at Trick 3, go across with a club and play four rounds of that suit. Both the defenders follow to all the clubs and you ruff the fourth round in hand. You next cash the ace-king of diamonds and cross to dummy with a trump. At this point, you pause to count the hand. Indeed, assuming nobody leads the ♡10 from 10-x-x, you know the exact distribution: West must have started with a 4-2-3-4 shape. This means you would incur an overruff if you were to ruff another heart. Thankfully, you can cater for the actual layout:

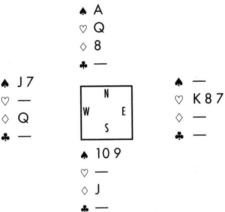

```
                    ♠ A
                    ♡ Q
                    ◇ 8
                    ♣ —
   ♠ J 7                             ♠ —
   ♡ —           ┌─────────┐        ♡ K 8 7
   ◇ Q           │    N    │        ◇ —
   ♣ —           │ W     E │        ♣ —
                 │    S    │
                 └─────────┘
                    ♠ 10 9
                    ♡ —
                    ◇ J
                    ♣ —
```

You play the ♡Q, discarding a diamond from hand. West cannot gain by ruffing and, with East obliged to return a heart, your 'sure' trump loser vanishes — a classic smother play.

Note that if you had reason to place West with a 4-3-3-3 shape, you would ruff a heart instead at the point you ruffed a club; you would then exit with a club at Trick 11 and still smother the ♠J. If you thought West was 4-3-2-4, you would ruff a heart in the diagrammed position, leaving West's trump winner and East's good diamond to fall on the same trick.

HAND 54 SAFETY SUCCESS

By paying close attention to the spade spots, yes you can make 3NT as the cards lie. After winning the initial heart, you cash the ♠K and note the fall of the ten on your right. You continue with the five, planning to run it if you get the chance. West correctly covers and you have to expend dummy's ace. When East shows out, perhaps throwing a heart, you know to abandon spades for the moment. It would be a mistake at this point to play ace and another club as that could reduce your options for the endgame. Instead, you duck a club and, no matter which defender wins this, you hold up the ◇A until the third round, discarding two clubs from dummy. Having regained the lead, you check for a 2-2 club break by playing a club to the ace. You do not get this, but this second round of clubs brings a bonus:

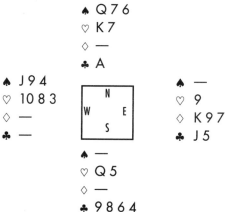

```
                    ♠ Q 7 6
                    ♡ K 7
                    ◇ —
                    ♣ A
      ♠ J 9 4                          ♠ —
      ♡ 10 8 3         N               ♡ 9
      ◇ —          W       E           ◇ K 9 7
      ♣ —              S               ♣ J 5
                    ♠ —
                    ♡ Q 5
                    ◇ —
                    ♣ 9 8 6 4
```

Since a spade discard would enable you to set up a long spade, we assume West throws a heart on this trick. However, this allows you to cash the ♡Q, cross back to the ♡K, and lead the six (or seven) of spades off dummy. West wins with the nine but must then surrender the last two tricks by leading from the ♠J. You manage to make a fourth spade trick after all!

Note that double dummy there are other winning lines. For example, you could duck a diamond at the point you gave up a club. In that case, you would lose a heart more and a club less.

HAND 55 STYLISH SEESAW

After knocking out the spade ace , winning the club return in dummy and playing a heart to the king, you must win the second round of clubs in hand. If you decided to overtake, you would face an impossible choice of whether to cash two spade winners, setting up the ten for East, or leaving one of them stranded, never to make. Instead, you should win the third round of clubs on the table and watch your opponent's discard expectantly. If a heart appears, you cash one spade and then play a heart off dummy. If East prefers to release a spade, you simply cash your black-suit winners.

As you may have guessed, East does better to duck the first spade lead. You dare not play a second to drive out the ace, as then you will get a third one back. Therefore, you play a heart to the king and must now tackle clubs. Moreover, you need to do so in such a way as to give yourself a choice of where to win the fourth round depending upon which suit East discards on the third.

You can cash the king, then play the jack to the queen (you know they have to break 3-2 anyway), and call for the ace:

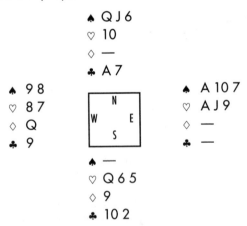

♠ Q J 6
♥ 10
♦ —
♣ A 7

♠ 9 8   ♠ A 10 7
♥ 8 7   ♥ A J 9
♦ Q   ♦ —
♣ 9   ♣ —

♠ —
♥ Q 6 5
♦ 9
♣ 10 2

If East pitches a spade, you drop the ten and knock out the ♠A; then the ♣7 serves as an entry back to the table. If the defender chooses to let go a heart, you follow with the ♣2 and lead a heart off dummy to set up two tricks in your hand. Bravo!

HAND 56 DOUBLE TAKE

After counting your winners carefully — five trumps, two diamonds, one heart and two clubs — you conclude that you need an endplay and a squeeze. Okay, this will depend on a bit of luck, but correct play deserves some.

If three diamonds (other than precisely 9-8-6) lie on your left, you are never going to succeed. For one thing, West will have a safe exit card in diamonds no matter how many rounds of them you cash. For another, with the clubs 4-4, the defenders will be able to share responsibility for protecting the suit.

You must play West for a doubleton diamond. In addition, you need to hope these are not both small cards because the twin entry position in diamonds has to stay intact for the second part of the plan — to squeeze East in the red suits. Correct timing, to cater for a possible ♣Q-x of clubs, runs as follows: unblock the ♣K, cash two more spades, then play the ♣A and ruff a heart before exiting with a trump:

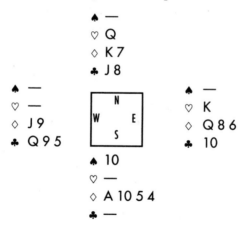

West should lead the ◇J here, hoping East has ◇Q-10-x (or that you misguess), but you can call for dummy's king and finesse the ten next. If instead West tries a low club, up goes the jack and East has no answer as you ruff a club to hand. The ♣Q exit comes to much the same thing. In that case, you ruff, cross to the ◇K and this time the ♣J serves as the squeeze card.

HAND 57 SECOND NATURE

Having won the first trick with the ♠J, East should have taken more care over the return. Would any decent player duck a spade with a heart loser off the top? In any case, South really needs the ♡A to justify an opening bid. A club switch, attacking dummy's entry in the suit, seems called for. West withholds the king and, from then on, the contract stands no real chance.

Sometimes it can work to your disadvantage to see all four hands. At the table, you would surely want to take the first trick for fear of a spade ruff. Besides, winning the first trick denies East the opportunity to kill dummy's club entry. At Trick 2 you must unblock the ♡A, then use the ace and jack of trumps as entries to ruff hearts: you want to isolate the heart guard with West. Now running the trumps produces this position:

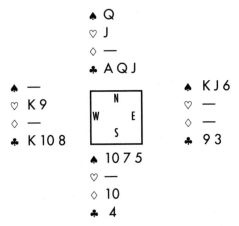

On the ◇10, West must release a heart to prevent you from taking the club finesse to wrap up three tricks in the suit. Once the defender has trimmed down to one heart, you throw the ♠Q from dummy and finesse the club. Finally, you concede a heart and await a club lead to enable you to repeat the club finesse.

By the way, you could still make the slam on an initial club lead. You would take the finesse and have a choice of whether to throw West in with a heart or endplay East in spades.

HAND 58 MOMENTARY MADNESS

After the seemingly obvious start to the hand — ◊K, ♣K, diamond ducked, diamond to the queen and ace — declarer can succeed. East's ◊2 return at Trick 2 strongly suggests a 5-4 diamond break, which means losing the lead will prove fatal. Therefore, the correct play is to test for a 3-3 spade break before touching a second round of clubs. This fails to turn up, but the actual split appears revealing. Holding just one spade, West surely has heart length. If the ♣A lies there as well, a third round of spades will exert intolerable pressure:

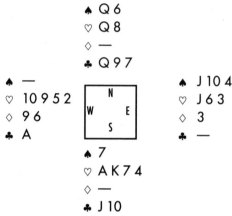

Assuming the first spade went to the king and the second came back to the ace, South will lead here, but it does not actually matter. West, who could spare a club on the second spade, faces an impossible choice. A heart discard costs a trick directly and throwing the ♣A would be even worse. However, letting a diamond go fails to save the day. Now that West has only one winning diamond left, declarer can knock out the ♣A; East can never get in to make any spade tricks.

To beat 3NT East must do something very odd: hang on to the ◊Q. Now the non-material squeeze falls flat because this defender will win the fourth round of diamonds and cash two good spades. Nor does playing a second round of clubs work: West grabs the ace whilst East discards the blocking ◊Q!

HAND 59 SOUTHERLY WIND

Suppose the ◊K wins the first trick, and that on four rounds of clubs West throws two spades and a heart whilst one heart goes from dummy. Declarer then proceeds to cash three rounds of spades and West comes under pressure. In order to prevent declarer from setting up a heart trick simply by ducking one round, West has to keep three hearts, which means releasing a diamond. After that declarer cashes the queen and ace of diamonds, leaving the lead in the South hand as planned. Finally, a low heart lead at Trick 11 obliges West to play high and then return a heart into the split tenace.

If West abandons diamonds earlier, will this break the slam? If the play follows similar lines to the previous paragraph, it will. After finishing the clubs, declarer needs to play two rounds of diamonds to elicit a spade discard from West. This succeeds, but a logistical problem arises. The ace-king-queen of spades take the next three tricks, meaning the lead stays in dummy for Trick 11.

To cater for the chance that West has kept four spades, declarer should throw a spade from dummy on the fourth club. This makes it possible to reach this position:

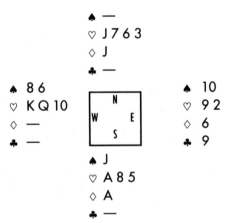

A diamond played to the ace now brings West down to one spade. Just as importantly, it puts the lead in the South hand. The ♠J followed by the ♡5 now lands the contract.

HAND 60 KNOCKOUT MOVE

If you recall, the early play ran as follows: ◊A, ♠A, heart to the ten, spade ruff, heart to the jack, spade ruff. Now what happens if declarer plays two trumps, throwing a spade from dummy?

East can spare a low club on the last trump. Declarer can duck a club, aiming to set up dummy's ♣Q, but the defender lies one step ahead. Having won the first club, East returns the ◊Q to knock out the ace, and can claim the last three tricks.

To bring off the endplay you need to find a way to reduce East's diamond length to the same length as yours and dummy's or make the cost of not doing so prohibitive. You can achieve this goal by an unusual technique, known as a 'knockout' squeeze. After the second round of spades, go back over with the ◊K and observe the effect of ruffing a third spade:

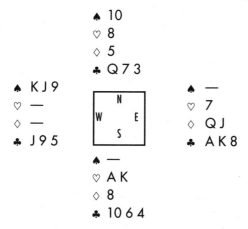

Can you see why club discard on the ♠10 will clearly prove fatal? This time you have the tempo to establish a club because you can discard a diamond on this trick and oblige West to attack the suit. Ruffing works no better; you overruff and it is now just like having a 2-2 trump break: you exit with a diamond and East must break the clubs or concede a ruff and discard. Lastly, if the defender discards a diamond, you ruff, draw the outstanding trump and play a diamond. There is little guesswork involved here because the bidding and opening lead rather mark East with five diamonds.

HAND 61 DIG DEEP

The fact that dummy contains the ♡A, East's potential exit suit, means you can eliminate hearts without ruffing — running trumps should do it. This is just as well since you lack the entries to ruff hearts three times. You should unblock the spades and cross to hand with the ♣K, noting that both defenders follow low. Next, you draw the last trump, and West doubtless discards a heart.

If East has ♣Q-10-9 left, you can run all but one trump, cross to the ♡A, ruff a heart and duck a club. A similar strategy deals with an original ♣Q-10-9-x-x. Whether East keeps three high clubs or two high and one low, you will have a throw-in position. Now watch what happens on the actual layout:

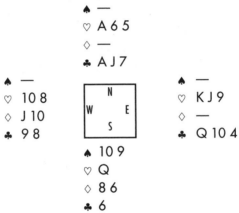

On the ♠10, West cannot spare a diamond, as you could set up your last one. Perhaps that defender prefers to pitch a heart. In that case, you might do best to throw a heart from dummy, forcing East to do likewise; then you cross to the ♡A and lead a heart, planning to throw a diamond. Lastly, if West discards the ♣8, a heart goes from dummy and again East must maintain parity with the table's club length to stop you ruffing out the suit. This time you should cross to the ♡A, ruff a heart and lead a club. When the nine appears, dummy's jack covers and East has no answer. If you go with the odds and play for hearts 4-4 rather than 5-3, there is no defensive strategy to thwart you.

HAND 62 MAGIC FORCE

Once West shows out on the second round of trumps, two issues present themselves. Firstly, you need to find a safe route to the South hand to pull the last trump. Secondly, you must leave open the chance to restrict your losses in the black suits to one by means of an endplay or squeeze on West.

You can play a third round of trumps, come to hand with the ♣K and draw the outstanding trump. The snag is that West can afford to come down to three clubs because you lack a way to get back to the long club. You can throw a heart from dummy and cash the ace-queen of clubs to eliminate the suit, but where do you go from there? If West started with ♠Q-10-9-8-6 or has pitched the three from ♠Q-10-9-8-3, you could duck a spade. However, that does not work today and nor would cashing the ♠A first: West wins the second spade cheaply and returns the ♠Q. The solution for Trick 5 is to overtake the ♣Q with the king! The trick soon comes back. Here is the position as you lead the ◇J:

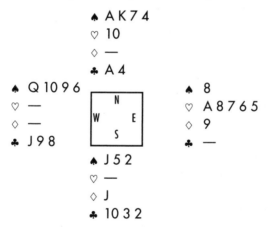

```
              ♠ A K 7 4
              ♡ 10
              ◇ —
              ♣ A 4
  ♠ Q 10 9 6      N        ♠ 8
  ♡ —                      ♡ A 8 7 6 5
  ◇ —        W       E     ◇ 9
  ♣ J 9 8          S       ♣ —
              ♠ J 5 2
              ♡ —
              ◇ J
              ♣ 10 3 2
```

You discard a heart from dummy and, if West has thrown a club, play a spade to the ace (in case of a bare ♠Q) and two rounds of clubs. The defender must lead a spade into the split tenace, allowing both your ♠J and long club to score. A spade discard produces a similar result. Three rounds of the suit set up the fourth spade and force West to concede a trick to your ♣10.

Running all the trumps will hardly work. If you decide to keep two diamonds, two spades and a heart in your hand, West does the same. You can cash three rounds of spades but, whether or not you take the ◇A first, there is no second squeeze. If you prefer to keep three spades and one card in each red suit, either a spade or diamond discard protects West from further pressure.

To succeed you need to play the hand as a trump squeeze, leaving a trump in dummy. Against very good players you may have to guess the ending because you lack a count on the pointed suits, but for practical purposes you can normally get here:

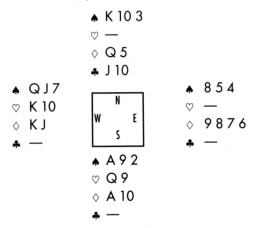

```
              ♠ K 10 3
              ♡ —
              ◇ Q 5
              ♣ J 10
 ♠ Q J 7                      ♠ 8 5 4
 ♡ K 10          N            ♡ —
 ◇ K J       W       E        ◇ 9 8 7 6
 ♣ —             S            ♣ —
              ♠ A 9 2
              ♡ Q 9
              ◇ A 10
              ♣ —
```

On the ♣J, you must throw the ◇10 from hand, even though it now blocks the suit. West faces a three-way choice of poisons. A diamond discard is the easiest to cope with. You come to the ◇A, ruff a heart and cash the ◇Q, throwing a spade to squeeze West in the majors. If instead the ♡10 appears at Trick 7, you use two aces as entries to ruff a heart and then cash the queen. This catches West in a positional simple squeeze. Finally, you deal with the awkward spade discard by taking three rounds of spades, ensuring the nine wins the third. West can then either throw a heart, allowing you to set up the ♡Q with a ruff, or pitch a diamond, enabling you to cash the ◇A to leave dummy high.

HAND 64 CLASH OF WILLS

Sometimes a defender can break up a squeeze by holding a winner back and so preventing declarer from rectifying the count. West's fifth club certainly limits how many rounds of clubs you can safely play. However, ducking both the second and third round of clubs gives you a choice of winning lines. After testing the hearts, it becomes clear that East has had to come down to a doubleton spade; so you cash two spades and exit with the fourth diamond for a heart return into the tenace. Alternatively, you can play four rounds of hearts; then, when you cash two more diamond winners, West will be squeezed in the black suits.

Winning the third round of clubs and exiting with the ◊ 8 presents the greatest challenge to declarer. Even if you already cashed two hearts to discover their layout, you cannot now get dummy's spades out of the way. Whilst this precludes a simple squeeze, look what happens if you cash your last club:

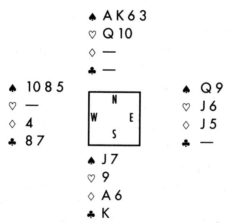

East has been able to come down to a doubleton spade since West guards the suit, but a further spade pitch would prove fatal. For example, you can simply cross to the ace, felling the queen as you do so, come back to the ♠ J and cash the ◊ A to leave the table high. Clearly East fares no better by discarding from one of the red suits. In each case, doing so would set up a fourth-round winner. This is a clash squeeze, no less.

HAND 65 DELAYING TACTICS

West has three suits to protect, but rattling off all your trumps does not work. Yes, to keep a diamond the defender will trim down to two spades or a lone ♣K, but you cannot derive much advantage from it. That exit card in diamonds proves your undoing.

You might think to try a spade towards the queen after you finish drawing trumps. If West flies in the king, any return should aid your cause. If not, dummy's queen wins and you can ruff a diamond to hand. Alas, running a string of hearts will still fail. West throws a club on the third round of trumps, a spade on the fourth and a club on the fifth. You can set up a club by leading low, but the wretch still has a diamond to play to East's winners.

To succeed you need to delay the diamond ruff. West can spare a club on the third trump and is then forced to discard a spade on the fourth. Now play the fifth:

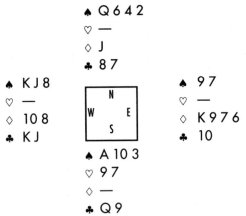

```
                  ♠ Q 6 4 2
                  ♡ —
                  ◇ J
                  ♣ 8 7
  ♠ K J 8          ┌─────────┐        ♠ 9 7
  ♡ —              │    N    │        ♡ —
  ◇ 10 8        W  │         │  E     ◇ K 9 7 6
  ♣ K J            │    S    │        ♣ 10
                  └─────────┘
                  ♠ A 10 3
                  ♡ 9 7
                  ◇ —
                  ♣ Q 9
```

West cannot afford to release another spade, as then you could play ace and another to set up both the queen and a long spade. A club discard proves equally fatal, although you must take care. Either keep two clubs in dummy or play spades next. In practice, West throws the ◇8. You get rid of a club from dummy, cross with the ♠10 to the ♠Q as West holds up, and ruff a diamond. Finally, you achieve the throw in with the third round of spades.

HAND 66 DRAWING TRUMPS!

With the heart position as it stands, you cannot easily arrange a throw in. If you try to run the eight, East will cover with the nine. If you know about the one-suit squeeze, this heart layout may ring a bell. If you can reduce everyone to three hearts, West will surely have to choose whether to retain the K-J-10 or the K-J and a low heart. You might be able to cope with either: you duck to smoke out the K-J-10, and run the eight if the jack or ten has gone. The snag is that you can only run the eight at Trick 11 if you won Trick 10 in dummy. Therein lies the crux of the hand.

You can never win the second diamond in dummy, and asking to take the last trump over there sounds a tall order. Even so, it can be done after the initial spade lead. Use the ◊K and middle trumps as entries to ruff three more spades and you get this:

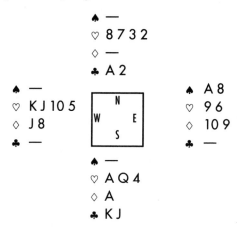

To avoid undoing the hard work, cash the ◊A before playing another trump. If West throws the ♡J, overtake with dummy's ace and lead the ♡8, planning to let it ride. Whether or not East covers, West will have to lead into a heart tenace or concede a ruff and discard. If West prefers to throw a diamond, you win this club in hand and the next one in dummy to effect the endplay. Finally, you can deal with the ♡5 discard by winning Trick 10 in either hand and ducking a heart. The hand was reasonably simple after all: you just had to draw trumps ending in dummy!

HAND 67 GUARDED PROGNOSIS

West ought to work out from the play to Trick 1 that South has the ◇A, otherwise East would surely overtake. This makes the diamond continuation futile. Of course, West cannot attack the spade threat: leading the jack would set up a finesse position whilst leading low would leave the jack bare. East's jump to 4♡ should make finding the heart shift painless. Now the spotlight moves across the table. East may play a second heart or revert to diamonds, but neither move beats the contract. Declarer scores the ◇A and runs trumps to reach this position:

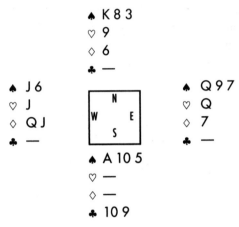

West can spare a diamond and dummy a spade but East is forced to abandon one of the red suits. The last trump then gives both defenders a problem. If East has kept a heart, West must throw one now, exposing East to a simple squeeze in the majors after dummy's diamond goes away. It comes to much the same thing if East keeps a diamond. Still forced to save ♠J-x to prevent a finesse, West discards a diamond at Trick 10. This time dummy releases a heart and East is squeezed in the pointed suits.

As we have discovered, the guard squeeze works equally well with one loser or two. There is only one safe way to break it up. After getting in with the ♡A, East switches to the ♠9, taking a backward finesse against South's ten. 5♣ must then fail.

HAND 68 MAGNIFICENT RESISTANCE

After the passive trump return at Trick 2 you were unable to evade the subsequent endplay because you lacked the means to give partner the lead. Somehow, you need to create an exit card for yourself. As you have seen, the final position is tricky enough to defend on the layout as it stands. Surely if you put declarer with the ♡Q, making dummy's hearts into a second tenace, it would become impossible. It will not work if South holds three hearts, but a switch to the ♡K surely offers the best hope. With four potential top losers, your opponent has to take this with dummy's ace. Now see if you can survive repeated trump leads. As before, you can throw one small heart, two clubs and the ◊J (actually even the ◊A) without reference to what dummy does.

Here is the ending with two trump tricks left:

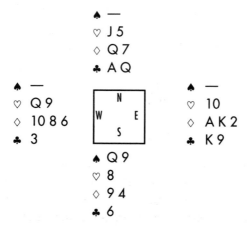

West can spare the ◊6 (or a club), and let us first suppose that a heart goes from dummy. In this case, you can now pitch any of your diamonds. On the final trump, West needs to keep two winning hearts and ideally throws away a club. Declarer does best to pitch the ♡J from dummy, whereupon you throw another diamond. Your side then has two hearts and a diamond to cash.

If declarer prefers to get rid of dummy's ◊7 at Trick 8, you adopt a different strategy. You throw the ♡10 and a big diamond on the last two trumps in either order. Can you see the result?

With dummy's ◊Q either bare or gone altogether, your side makes two diamonds and one heart at the end. This is just as good as taking two hearts and a diamond.

At the table, there is a danger you might spot the ♡K switch a trick too late. If you cash a high diamond first, the contract rolls in. Shall we double check?

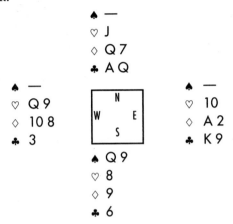

On declarer's last two trumps it is easy to see that you will have to part with your two potential exit cards: the ♡10 and the ◊2. You will then be thrown in with a diamond. Whilst many players would find it hard to foresee the precise ending back at Trick 2, a general rule helps: in a three suit situation, declarer can achieve a strip via a squeeze either if the main defender has no means of exit or if just two losers remain. Before you cashed the diamond, declarer had three losers; after it, only two.

You may have noticed that an initial diamond lead would have beaten the contract more easily. You could then have played three rounds of the suit straight away. Mind you, if one turns back the clock, North might call 3NT instead of 4♠!

Finally, in case you are interested, 4♠ could always be made if South held a 7-1-2-3 or 7-2-1-3 shape. It could also be made after the initial club lead if South were 7-1-3-2 or 7-3-1-2. In both cases, it would take a lead in declarer's red-suit fragment to defeat it. It may relieve you to hear that a shortage of space prevents a full analysis of these points!

More Bridge Titles from Master Point Press

Bridge Problems for a New Millennium by Julian Pottage
160 pp., PB   Can $14.95   US $11.95

Bridge the Silver Way by David Silver and Tim Bourke
192 pp., PB   Can $19.95   US $14.95

Bridge Squeezes for Everyone* *Yes, even you!* by David Bird
220 pp., PB   Can $24.95   US $17.95

Bridge: 25 Steps to Learning 2/1
by Paul Thurston (foreword by Eric Kokish)
192 pp., PB   Can $19.95   US $15.95

25 Ways to Take More Tricks as Declarer
by Barbara Seagram and David Bird
200 pp., PB   Can $19.95   US $15.95

Bridge: 25 Ways to Compete in the Bidding.
by Barbara Seagram and Marc Smith
220 pp., PB   Can $19.95   US $15.95

Bridge, Zia... and me
by Michael Rosenberg (foreword by Zia Mahmood)
192 pp., PB   Can $19.95   US $15.95

Challenge Your Declarer Play by Danny Roth
128 pp., PB   Can $12.95   US $ 9.95

Classic Kantar *a collection of bridge humor* by Eddie Kantar
192 pp., PB   Can $19.95   US $14.95

Competitive Bidding in the 21st Century by Marshall Miles
254 pp., PB   Can $22.95   US. $16.95

Countdown to Winning Bridge by Tim Bourke and Marc Smith
192 pp., PB   Can $19.95   US $14.95

Easier Done Than Said *Brilliancy at the Bridge Table*
by Prakash K. Paranjape
128 pp., PB   Can $15.95   US $12.95

Eddie Kantar Teaches Topics in Declarer Play by Eddie Kantar
128 pp., PB   Can $27.95   US $19.95

For Love or Money *The Life of a Bridge Journalist*
by Mark Horton and Brian Senior
189 pp., PB   Can $22.95   US $16.95

Following the LAW by Larry Cohen
192 pp., PB   Can $19.95   US $15.95

Focus On Declarer Play by Danny Roth
128 pp., PB   Can $12.95   US $9.95

Focus On Defence by Danny Roth
128 pp., PB   Can $12.95   US $9.95

Focus On Bidding by Danny Roth
160 pp., PB   Can $14.95   US $11.95

How to Play Bridge with Your Spouse... and Survive!
by Roselyn Teukolsky
192 pp., PB   Can $19.95   US $14.95

I Shot my Bridge Partner by Matthew Granovetter
384 pp., PB   Can $19.95   US $14.95

Inferences at Bridge by Marshall Miles
192 pp., PB   Can $22.95   US $16.95

Larry Cohen's Bidding Challenge by Larry Cohen
192 pp., PB   Can $19.95   US $15.95

Murder at the Bridge Table by Matthew Granovetter
320 pp., PB   Can $19.95   US $14.95

Partnership Bidding *a workbook* by Mary Paul
96 pp., PB   Can $9.95   US $7.95

Playing with the Bridge Legends by Barnet Shenkin
(forewords by Zia and Michael Rosenberg)
240 pp., PB   Can $24.95   US $17.95

The Pocket Guide to Bridge by Barbara Seagram and Ray Lee
64 pp., PB   Can $9.95   US $7.95

Richelieu Plays Bridge by Robert F. MacKinnon
220 pp., PB   Can $24.95   US $17.95

Saints and Sinners *The St. Titus Bridge Challenge*
by David Bird & Tim Bourke
192 pp., PB   Can $19.95   US $14.95

Samurai Bridge *A tale of old Japan* by Robert F. MacKinnon
256 pp., PB   Can $ 22.95   US $16.95

Tales out of School *'Bridge 101' and other stories*
by David Silver (foreword by Dorothy Hayden Truscott)
128 pp., PB   Can $ 12.95   US $9.95

The Bridge Magicians
by Mark Horton and Radoslaw Kielbasinski
248 pp., PB   Can $24.95   US $17.95

The Bridge Player's Bedside Book edited by Tony Forrester
256 pp., HC   Can $27.95   US $19.95

The Bridge World's 'Test Your Play' by Jeff Rubens
164 pp., PB   Can.$14.95   US $11.95

The Complete Book of BOLS Bridge Tips
edited by Sally Brock
176 pp., PB (photographs)   Can $24.95   US$17.95

There Must Be A Way... *52 challenging bridge*
hands by Andrew Diosy (foreword by Eddie Kantar)
96 pp., PB   Can $9.95   US $9.95

Thinking on Defense *The art of visualization at bridge*
by Jim Priebe
197 pp., PB   Can $ 19.95   US $15.95

To Bid or Not to Bid by Larry Cohen
248 pp., PB   Can $24.95   US $17.95

You Have to See This... *52 more challenging bridge problems*
by Andrew Diosy and Linda Lee
96 pp., PB   Can $12.95   US $9.95

Win the Bermuda Bowl with Me
by Jeff Meckstsroth and Marc Smith
188 pp., PB   Can $24.95   US $17.95

World Class — *conversations with the bridge masters*
by Marc Smith
288 pp., PB (photographs)   Can $24.95   US $17.95